1 AND 2 PETER BIBLE STUDY

PRACTICAL TEACHING AND PROFOUND
INSIGHTS FROM PETER'S LETTERS TO JESUS'S
CHURCH

40-DAY BIBLE STUDY SERIES
BOOK 13

PETER DEHAAN

1 and 2 Peter Bible Study: Practical Teaching and Profound Insights from Peter's Letters to Jesus's Church

Copyright © 2025 by Peter DeHaan.

40-Day Bible Study Series, Book 13

Library of Congress Control Number: 2025900027

Published by Rock Rooster Books, Grand Rapids, Michigan

ISBNs:

- 979-8-88809-113-5 (ebook)
- 979-8-88809-114–2 (paperback)
- 979-8-88809-115-9 (hardcover)
- 979-8-88809-116-6 (audiobook)

Credits:

- Developmental editor: Julie Harbison
- Copyeditor: Robyn Mulder
- Cover design: Fanderclai Design
- Author photo: Chelsie Jensen Photography

To Elle

Series by Peter DeHaan

40-Day Bible Study Series takes a fresh and practical look into Scripture, book by book.

Bible Character Sketches Series celebrates people in Scripture, from the well-known to the obscure.

Holiday Celebration Bible Study Series rejoices in the holidays with Jesus.

Visiting Churches Series takes an in-person look at church practices and traditions to inform and inspire today's followers of Jesus.

Be the first to hear about Peter's new books and receive updates at PeterDeHaan.com/updates.

CONTENTS

WHO IS PETER?

Peter is one of Jesus's twelve disciples. His birth name was Simon, but later Jesus gives him the new name of Peter (Cephas). *Peter* means "stone" or "rock." We'll get back to this in a bit.

Peter is a part of Jesus's inner circle of three, along with James and John. As such, he receives a privileged look into who Jesus is and what he does.

Despite this, Peter often receives criticism—even ridicule—for his behavior. He sometimes speaks or acts before he thinks.

During Jesus's arrest, Peter whips out a sword and slashes at someone, but all he gets is an ear (Luke 22:49–51). After that, Peter denies even knowing Jesus (Matthew 26:69–75).

But let's not focus on these things. Let's look at the positive, for there is much to celebrate.

Peter is the only one of the twelve disciples who walks on water (Matthew 14:28–33). Though his journey is short before his faith falters, remember that he's the only one to leave the safety of the boat. The other eleven don't even dare try. Peter does, and his faith is rewarded.

When Jesus asks his disciples, "What do people say about me?" they give various answers. Then Jesus gets direct. "What do *you* say?"

Not surprisingly, Peter speaks first. His bold answer fills us with confidence: "You're the Messiah, the Son of the living God" (Matthew 16:15–19).

Jesus blesses Peter for his spot-on answer. This truth sets the foundation for Jesus's church. That's when Jesus changes the disciple's name from Simon to Peter—which means rock—the rock on which Jesus will build his church.

After Jesus rises from the dead and returns to heaven, Peter emerges as the church's first leader (Acts 1:15–26). Peter speaks on Pentecost under the power of the Holy Spirit. Three thousand people believe in Jesus (Acts 2:14–41).

Later, people lay the sick on the streets so that

Peter's shadow might fall on them as he walks by (Acts 5:15). Though the Bible never says these folks receive healing, why would their friends position them this way if there wasn't a good reason to do so?

Last, Peter writes two letters to Jesus's followers, which we can read in the New Testament: 1 Peter and 2 Peter. This Bible study digs into these two letters.

Like all of us, Peter has his strengths and his weaknesses. May we seek to emulate the positive parts of Peter's example and avoid the negative.

Would we have walked on water with Peter or stayed in the boat with the other disciples? What in Peter's life can inform how we live ours?

[Discover more about Peter in Mark 9:2–8, Mark 14:32–41, John 21:15–19, and Acts 3:1–10.]

1 PETER

Peter wrote a letter to Jesus's followers, that is, to God's elect. We can read this letter—also called an epistle—in the book of 1 Peter in the Bible.

Unlike Paul's letters, which contain targeted instructions to specific churches or individuals, 1 Peter (and 2 Peter) are general instructions to all believers. As such, they carry a common appeal and offer universal application for all Christians everywhere.

The audience of 1 Peter is primary Gentile (that is non-Hebrew) converts who follow Jesus. First, Peter helps them connect their Christian beliefs to its roots in Jewish history, as seen in the Old

Testament. The result is a deeper, more holistic comprehension of their faith foundation.

Be aware that a recurring theme in this book is suffering. This concept is antithetical to the popular but erroneous notion that following Jesus will make life easy. Know that the Bible doesn't teach this. In truth, we may suffer for our Christian faith, but the rewards for persevering are even greater.

Overall, however, 1 Peter is a warm and attractive read that is ideal for those who have just begun following Jesus. Yet it's equally instructive—if not more so—for seasoned believers.

Some people dismiss Peter's letter because of its many instructions on how to act, claiming it promotes salvation through works. Yet they misunderstand. Peter writes to Jesus's church, to those who already follow him and have received their salvation through faith. As such, we should want to change our behavior in response to what Jesus has done and not to earn what we've already received.

Overall, 1 Peter overflows with practical insights and fundamental truths. May we receive much through his words to guide and encourage us on our faith journey with Jesus.

Do we expect Jesus to take away all our problems and make life easy? Where are we on the spectrum of new believer to seasoned follower of Jesus?

[Discover more about Peter, suffering, and God's protection in Acts 4:1–20 and Acts 12:1–18.]

DAY 1: LIVING IN EXILE
1 PETER 1:1

To God's elect, exiles scattered throughout the provinces of Pontus, Galatia, Cappadocia, Asia and Bithynia. (1 Peter 1:1)

Peter opens his letter identifying the recipients. It's a multi-part identifier with the first two elements appearing in verse one. First, they're God's elect, his chosen people. We'll cover this in tomorrow's reading, and we'll see it throughout the rest of his letter.

The other element—and our focus for today's reading—is that they are exiles. Other translations call them foreigners, strangers, sojourners, pilgrims, and even aliens. The point is that they aren't where they belong. They're God's people, living far from home in a pagan culture. (Consider Lot's situation, 2 Peter 2:7–9.)

As exiles, they differ from the unsaved locals. They stand out. They look differently, talk differently, and behave differently. It's obvious that they don't belong. Yet they're there, anyway.

In the same way, we are exiles, or at least we should be. As God's children here on earth, we, too, live in a foreign culture among pagans. We look differently, talk differently, and behave differently. Or at least we should if we make following Jesus a priority. As such, it's obvious that we don't belong here, yet we're here anyway.

What should our reaction be?

Do we try to blend in and hide our distinctiveness? Or are we content—even intentional—to stand out for Jesus?

As we stand out, may we stand out for God-honoring ideals. May others know us for our virtue, our integrity, and our righteousness. May we live an exemplary life for Jesus, revealing our faith and showing his love.

As spiritual exiles, our home is not here. We're merely passing through. We look forward to our eternal home, our destination with Jesus in heaven.

May Jesus be our focus during our time here on earth as exiles.

Let's be bold in telling others about Jesus. Then they may follow him and join us in spending eternity with him.

How well do we do at embracing the idea that we're exiles here on earth? What can we do to better let our distinctiveness as Jesus's followers stand out for others to see?

[Discover more about being an exile in 1 Peter 2:11. Read about being foreigners in Ephesians 2:11–20 and Hebrews 11:13.]

DAY 2: CHOSEN
1 PETER 1:2

. . . chosen according to the foreknowledge of God the Father, through the sanctifying work of the Spirit, to be obedient to Jesus Christ and sprinkled with his blood. (1 Peter 1:2)

As God's elect, we are a chosen people. Why are we chosen? It's not because of who we are or for what we've done. So we shouldn't think we're chosen because of our merit. We don't need to get God's attention for him to pick us. He already did. It's not something we must strive to get (Ephesians 2:8–10).

Expanding on this, let's look at the rest of this verse. We see the Trinity of the Father, Son, and

Holy Spirit identified as taking part in our election. Interestingly, they don't appear in that order, which is how we typically think of the Triune God. Instead, it's Father, Spirit, and Jesus.

First, it starts with us being chosen according to Father God's foreknowledge. Foreknowledge means that he knew of us prior to our existence. Before we were, he chose us. This truth should leave us in awe. He picked us in advance, before we did anything. We are his elect.

Next, we read of the Holy Spirit. The Holy Spirit works in us to sanctify us. Sanctify means that he sets us apart for sacred use, for God's purposes. He consecrates us, making us holy and pure. Again, this isn't something that we have to do. It's something that the Holy Spirit does in us. Yes, we should willingly cooperate with his sanctifying work, but it's not something we need to do—or even can do— apart from the Holy Spirit.

Notice that Peter doesn't say *sanctified*, as in something already done. Instead, the disciple says *sanctifying*. It's ongoing. This means we can expect the Holy Spirit's sanctifying work in us to continue throughout the rest of our lives, bringing us into closer alignment with the person God wants us to become. That is, of course, presuming we allow the Spirit to do so.

Once again, we don't need to sanctify ourselves to earn our right standing with God. Instead, our sanctification occurs *because* of our right standing with him.

Last, we see Jesus. Yet we shouldn't assume this means he's the least important. Everything hinges on him. He died on the cross as the sacrifice to cover all the wrong things we have done. That is, to atone for our sins.

As our dying Savior, his blood represents our salvation. As a way of thanking him for this ultimate gift of all gifts—one that lasts into eternity—we seek to obey him. This isn't a requirement for our salvation but the result of it. And it's the sanctifying work of the Holy Spirit that allows us to do so.

As a result, we give thanks to God the Father, the Spirit, and Jesus.

How can we better cooperate with the Holy Spirit's sanctifying work in us? How can we best show our appreciation to God for what he has done and is doing for us?

[Discover more about being chosen in Ephesians 1:11, Colossians 3:12, 1 Thessalonians 1:4, 1 Peter 2:9, and Revelation 17:14.]

DAY 3: LIVING HOPE THROUGH JESUS

1 PETER 1:3–5

In his great mercy he has given us new birth into a living hope through the resurrection of Jesus Christ from the dead.

(1 Peter 1:3)

With Peter's lengthy and theologically rich introduction to his letter complete, we now move into his main content.

Peter opens by praising Father God and our Lord Jesus. It's always wise to couch whatever we do with praise to our Creator and Savior. This is right because without our existence and our salvation, nothing else matters. Everything starts with God.

The first specific item in Peter's praise is God's

mercy. In simple terms, mercy is not getting the bad things we deserve. In this regard, mercy triumphs over the judgment that our actions warrant. Though not mentioned here, mercy works with grace. A simple definition of grace is getting good things that we don't deserve. God's mercy and God's grace complement each other.

Through God's mercy—and his grace—we receive a new birth through Jesus. We're born again (John 3:3–8). This comes through putting our faith and trust in Jesus when we follow him as our resurrected Savior. As a result, we have a living hope through Jesus.

Many people who accept Jesus as their Savior view it as an eternal reward. It's future focused. This means that when they die, their spirit will go into heaven and live there with Jesus forever. Eternity awaits them. This isn't a wrong perspective. It's correct, but it's also incomplete.

Our hope in Jesus and the salvation he provides is not only a future hope. It's a present hope too. This is why Peter calls it a living hope.

This living hope starts the day we say yes to following Jesus. It continues through our present life and carries us into the next one.

Being a Christian should be more—it is more—

than a get-out-of-hell card. It's not just a new life in heaven after we die. It's also a new life here on earth while we still live.

Following Jesus should inform how we live our life each day. May we strive to honor him through living a life worthy of all that he's done for us. We don't do this to garner his favor or earn our salvation; we do it as a way of joyfully thanking him for the salvation he's already given us.

What can we do to better thank Jesus for saving us? What are we doing in our life today to live out our hope through Jesus?

[Discover more about our hope in Jesus in 1 Peter 1:13, 1 Peter 1:21, and 1 Peter 3:15.]

DAY 4: BELIEVING WITHOUT SEEING
1 PETER 1:6–9

Though you have not seen him, you love him; and even though you do not see him now, you believe in him and are filled with an inexpressible and glorious joy. (1 Peter 1:8)

Faith is an interesting concept. It's a beautiful mystery. It comes to us in spurts. It is at times perplexing, even evasive. Sometimes we have faith and sometimes doubt creeps in.

What is faith? The writers of Hebrews tell us that faith is having confidence in what we hope for. It's the assurance of what we cannot see (Hebrews 11:1).

Given this, Peter implicitly celebrates the faith

of his audience. He says even though they have never seen Jesus, they love him anyway. Even though they don't see him now, they believe in him.

This reminds me of Jesus's disciple Thomas. Most people call him Doubting Thomas, but I view him as Realistic Thomas. His friends insist that the crucified and entombed Jesus is alive, but Thomas doesn't believe them. He demands proof. Though Jesus gives him the evidence he seeks, the Savior commends those who believe in his resurrection by faith alone (John 20:24–29).

So it is with us. By faith we believe in Jesus, follow him, and become his disciples. Though we have never seen him and don't see him now, we believe in him and who he is anyway. This is faith at its finest.

As a result, our faith in Jesus fills us with inexpressible joy, with a glorious joy.

Consider this for a moment.

We receive Jesus by faith as our Redeemer and our Savior. There's nothing we need to do or can do to earn our salvation. We just accept it—by faith.

Yet if we've been following Jesus for a long time, we may have lost our initial awe over this most wonderful gift of all gifts. (Consider Revelation 2:4.)

If so, it's time for us to recall his unsurpassed love for us and sacrificial death to cover all the wrong things we have done to make us right with Father God. As we remember this, may it fill us with an inexpressible and glorious joy.

But there's more.

In the next verse, Peter continues the thought about faith and joy. He reminds them—and us— that the result of our faith is the salvation of our souls (1 Peter 1:9).

This is most certainly something to celebrate.

What can we do to reclaim our awe over who Jesus is and what he did for us? When have we last thanked Jesus for giving us the greatest gift of all gifts?

[Discover more about faith in Romans 10:10 and Ephesians 2:8–9.]

DAY 5: HOLY SPIRIT SENT TO US
1 PETER 1:10–12

It was revealed to them that they were not serving themselves but you, when they spoke of the things that have now been told you by those who have preached the gospel to you by the Holy Spirit sent from heaven. (1 Peter 1:12)

The prophets of old were not serving themselves but others. The obvious recipients of their messages were the people who lived when they lived. They were the prophets' primary audience.

Yet future generations are the prophets' secondary audience. This group of people is a much larger one. Their numbers grow throughout time and have expanded to include you and me.

This means that the Old Testament prophets are, in effect, serving us today through the passage of time. We can read their words in the Bible, using them to inform us today and guide us on our faith journey.

We must remember, however, that these prophets don't speak to us on their own accord through human wisdom, grand vision, or writing prowess. They speak to us through the Holy Spirit, Father God's emissary sent to them from heaven.

The Holy Spirit is available to all of us today who follow Jesus. This, however, was not always the case. Prior to Jesus sending us this amazing guide, God's Spirit only came upon select individuals—the prophets, some judges, and a few kings. For some, this only happened in a specific instance or for a limited time.

But this is not true for us today.

Through Jesus we all have the Holy Spirit living within us. It's up to us, however, to recognize him, hear his words, and embrace his presence.

The Holy Spirit is not only present in us, but he's also present throughout the Bible. He appears in every book in the New Testament except for the brief letters of Philemon, 2 John, and 3 John. Not surprisingly, the Holy Spirit shows up most often in the book of Acts, which chronicles his essential role in the early church. And that role continues with us today.

If we want to learn more about the Holy Spirit, we can study him in Scripture. Even better would be to ask him to reveal himself to us. He can guide us, inspire us, and reveal supernatural truth to us.

All we need to do is to be open to receive what he has to say. Then we listen, and we obey.

Following the prophets' example, what are we doing to serve others, especially future generations? What role do we allow the Holy Spirit to play in our lives?

[Discover more about the Holy Spirit in Luke 24:45–49, John 14:26, John 20:21–23, and Acts 2:1–21.]

DAY 6: BE ALERT
1 PETER 1:13–16

Therefore, with minds that are alert and fully sober, set your hope on the grace to be brought to you when Jesus Christ is revealed at his coming. (1 Peter 1:13)

Today's passage opens with the word *therefore*. Whenever we see this word appear in Scripture (or any writing, for that matter), we must consider the preceding passage that it builds upon. A clever reminder to do this is that whenever we see the word *therefore*, we must look to see what it is *there for*.

The preceding passage talks about the prophets, the gospel—that is the good news of Jesus's salvation—and the Holy Spirit. This threefold witness should motivate us to follow what Peter tells us to do next. His instruction gives us three actions to obey, which immediately follows the connecting word of *therefore*.

First, we must keep our minds alert. This means to be vigilant to what's happening around us, to maintain our focus. To do so, we must remove distractions. This is necessary if we are to remain alert.

But what are we to be alert to? Though Peter doesn't specify it directly, we can glean some good ideas from the prior passage—the words that come before *therefore*. We should be alert to what we can learn from the prophets' message, for opportunities to tell others about Jesus, and to embrace the Holy Spirit's work in our lives.

Next is to be fully sober. This goes way beyond a call to avoid drunkenness. It's an imperative to shun anything that will impair our senses, to limit our awareness of what's happening around us. Other translations tell us to be sober-minded, self-disciplined, and exercise self-control. In doing these things, we stay on high alert for the opportunities God places before us.

Third, we are to set our hope on Jesus's grace, which we'll see fully revealed when he comes again.

Recall that grace is receiving the good things that we don't deserve. The epitome of grace is receiving salvation through Jesus. We don't deserve it, but he gives it to us anyway. This is grace at its finest.

We place our hope in this grace. But this hope is more than merely wishing for the best. It's a confident trust. The hope we have in Jesus should guide all that we do, the words we say, and the places we go. As we do this, we rely on the power of the Holy Spirit to make the most of every opportunity.

What must we do to keep our minds alert and fully sober? How can the hope we have in Jesus guide our actions and our words?

[Discover what else Peter has to say about this in 1 Peter 3:15–16.]

DAY 7: LIVE IN REVERENT FEAR
1 PETER 1:17–21

Since you call on a Father who judges each person's work impartially, live out your time as foreigners here in reverent fear. (1 Peter 1:17)

What ideas come to mind when you think about Father God? For me, it's love, grace, and mercy. The idea of reverent fear doesn't appear on my list, but it should. Peter says so.

The apostle tells us to live out our time as foreigners here on earth in reverent fear. The phrase *reverent fear* only occurs one other time in the Bible. It comes later in Peter's letter (1 Peter 2:18).

This reverent fear isn't a terrifying fear that

causes us to run away. Nor is it a petrifying fear that makes us freeze. It's also not a motivating fear that riles us up to fight. Instead, it's a respectful fear, one that evokes awe in who God is and his power.

The motivation for our reverent fear is because of God's judgment of our work. Peter confirms God's findings will be impartial, that is, unbiased. In this way, our Lord's objective nature rules out the potential for mercy, which means God's verdict will be just.

We deserve judgment from the Father for our sins, which are both numerous and overwhelming. That would be just, but Jesus already covered our sins when he died on the cross to make us right with Papa. Through Jesus, our sins are gone and forgotten (Hebrews 10:17–18, which quotes Jeremiah 31:34). As far as God is concerned, it's as if our sins never happened.

In considering this judgment, know that we don't need to do good things or perform God-honoring deeds to get our Lord's attention or earn his favor. We already have that. He loves us unconditionally, regardless of what we do or don't do. Since his love for us is absolute, there's nothing we can do to make it increase or nothing we will do to cause it to lessen.

Yet because of his love and his forgiveness, we should want to do things to honor him. Consider this as a way for us to say "thank you" to him for saving us.

Therefore, this judgment we will receive is for the work we do as Jesus's followers *after* he saves us. It doesn't earn our salvation, or guarantee it, because we're already in, regardless. Instead, we can view this judgment as God's way of affirming us for all the things we will do for him to give him glory, tell others about him, and grow his kingdom.

In this way, we see his judgment as a means for him to affirm all we've done for him. May his judgment of us produce a lengthy list worthy of celebration.

How can we have a reverent fear of God? Though there's a reason to look forward to his judgment of us, how well do we do at embracing it?

[Discover more about fear in 2 Corinthians 5:11, Philippians 2:12, and 1 John 4:18.]

DAY 8: PURIFIED THROUGH OBEDIENCE
1 PETER 1:22–25

Now that you have purified yourselves by obeying the truth so that you have sincere love for each other, love one another deeply, from the heart. (1 Peter 1:22)

In "Day 2: Chosen" we talked extensively about the sanctifying work of the Holy Spirit in us. To sanctify means that God sets us apart for sacred use, making us holy and pure. The result of our sanctification is to bring about our obedience to Jesus (1 Peter 1:2).

Peter now returns to this topic and says we're purified through our obedience when we obey the truth.

What is this truth that we need to obey?

Though Peter doesn't directly specify it, the context from the preceding passage suggests that it's the truth of Jesus's good news, of believing in him as our Savior.

Our obedience to this truth starts when we follow Jesus.

When we take this initial step, we become purified through him and his saving work of dying in our place to restore us into a right relationship with Father God. This begins our sanctification process. In a spiritual sense, our sanctification is complete because through Jesus we are holy and pure. (Theologians call this *positional sanctification*.)

Yet in the physical sense, our bodies aren't there yet. Our human self—despite having our sins forgiven—is not fully holy or completely pure. It's a work in progress. Our sanctification is ongoing. (Theologians call this *progressive sanctification*.)

This sanctification is a continual process that lasts throughout our life. Because of Jesus—and through the Holy Spirit—we become more set apart for sacred use, more holy, and more pure. Though we will never fully achieve these goals during our life here on earth, we will move toward them. In doing so, we become more like Jesus (Romans 8:29).

A key outcome of our ongoing sanctification is to develop a sincere love for others. The goal is for our love for others to increase, as of coming from deep inside our hearts. We strive to love people, just as Jesus loves us. A great guideline is to treat them in the same way that we want to be treated (Matthew 7:12), which is the essence of the Golden Rule.

Through Jesus, and because of Jesus, we are to love one another (John 13:34 and 1 John 3:23).

How are we becoming more sanctified as we follow Jesus? How can we more deeply love one another from the depths of our hearts?

[Discover more about God sanctifying us in 1 Thessalonians 4:3–6 and 1 Thessalonians 5:23.]

BONUS CONTENT: IMPERISHABLE SEED

For you have been born again, not of perishable seed, but of imperishable, through the living and enduring word of God.
(1 Peter 1:23)

I n "Day 3: Living Hope Through Jesus" we talked about our new birth in Jesus, of being born again. For a birth to occur, a seed must first be planted.

Biologically, the seed is one that will perish. It will one day die. It does not last. In contrast, the seed planted for our spiritual birth—to be born again—is imperishable. It lives on into eternity and will never die. It lasts forever—and so will we.

Our physical birth will one day end with our physical death. We will perish. In contrast, our spiritual birth will continue forever with a never-ending life. It will never perish.

Our bodies are temporal. Our spirits are eternal.

That's why we shouldn't concern ourselves with the things of the world. Instead, we should focus on the things of God.

Earlier in his letter, Peter reminded us we weren't redeemed by perishable things, such as gold or silver. This means we can't buy our salvation. Instead, we're redeemed through the death of Jesus, who serves as our sacrificial lamb—one without blemish or defect—offering himself as a perfect sacrifice, one that ends all sacrifices (1 Peter 1:18–19).

To accept the gift of his sacrifice and follow him is what it means to be born again.

Do we focus more on things that will perish or things that are imperishable? How does being born again influence our actions and our perspectives?

[Discover more about the imperishable in 1 Corinthians 15:42–3, 50, and 53.]

DAY 9: GROW IN SALVATION
1 PETER 2:1–3

Like newborn babies, crave pure spiritual milk, so that by it you may grow up in your salvation. (1 Peter 2:2)

The second chapter of Peter's letter opens with the word *therefore*. This handy reminder tells us to check the preceding passage to understand the context, which talks about being born again.

Because we are born again, we must, therefore, remove malice, deceit, hypocrisy, envy, and slander of every kind from our lives. Let's not rush past this list.

Malice is a desire to hurt others or see them

suffer. It's extreme ill will or being spiteful (see Psalm 5:9).

Deceit is the art or practice of causing deception. It's tricking people. It's a falseness (see Psalm 32:2).

Hypocrisy is acting in a way counter to what we claim to believe. It's saying one thing and doing another (see Psalm 26:4).

Envy wants what other people have. It's a discontentment over or a coveting of what someone else possesses, be it their station in life, their possessions, or what they've achieved (see Proverbs 14:30).

Slander is making false or malicious statements about another to hurt their reputation or to gain an advantage over them (see Psalm 101:5).

Because we are born again, we must remove—with all diligence—these five evils from our lives.

To help us do so, we should crave pure spiritual milk. Just as babies need their mother's milk to live, we, likewise, need spiritual milk if we are to flourish in our spiritual lives.

This reference to milk isn't merely a statement of need or a nice-to-have perspective. Instead, we must crave this milk. It's essential to our spiritual well-being. We must have it if we are to survive and grow.

We know how babies passionately suckle at their mother's breast or eagerly gulp a bottle of milk. In that moment, receiving that precious sustenance is all that matters to these babies. If anything interrupts their quest, they respond with cries of loud discontent, even anger.

So should it be with us when it comes to our pure spiritual milk.

Where do we find this pure spiritual milk?

A great place to start is Scripture. We need to read God's Word and hide it in our hearts (Psalm 119:11).

We can also receive pure spiritual milk as insight from the Holy Spirit (Luke 12:11–12 and John 14:26).

A third area is meaningful community with other like-minded believers (Hebrews 10:24–25).

May we passionately crave these things.

Which of the five items on Peter's list do we need to be more diligent about removing from our lives? How much do we crave pure spiritual milk?

[Discover more about spiritual growth in 1 Corinthians 3:6–7, Ephesians 4:15–16, and 2 Peter 3:18.]

DAY 10: LIVING STONES
1 PETER 2:4–8

You also, like living stones, are being built into a spiritual house to be a holy priesthood, offering spiritual sacrifices acceptable to God through Jesus Christ. (1 Peter 2:5)

Peter writes that we're built into a spiritual house as a holy priesthood to offer spiritual sacrifices (1 Peter 2:4–5). A parallel thought comes from Paul. He says that true and proper worship is to offer our bodies as living sacrifices (Romans 12:1).

First, Peter says we're living stones. As living stones, we are alive—not inanimate rocks. Jesus may have had this in mind in his rebuff of the Pharisees who took offense at the praise his followers gave him. The teacher tells them that if the crowd doesn't celebrate his arrival, the stones will cry out to exalt him (Luke 19:39–40). To do this, the rocks would have to come alive.

As Jesus's living stones, our actions matter. We live for Jesus. We exist to honor him, praise him, and glorify him. Our purpose is to tell others about him through our actions and through our words. Our faith is alive, and what we do must show it. In doing so, we help to advance his kingdom.

Next, as living stones, we're part of God's holy temple, a spiritual house (Ephesians 2:22). We become part of the construction of his new worship space.

If we're part of his spiritual temple, we don't need to go to church to meet him. This is because, as his temple, he's already in our presence, and we're already in his. This means we can experience him at anytime, anywhere. Through Jesus, God's temple exists everywhere we go. This should give us a fresh perspective about the idea of going to church.

As living stones, we are being made into a holy priesthood. If we are truly priests through what Jesus did for us, then we don't need ministers to point us to God, explain him to us, or assist us in encountering him. God is preparing us to do that for ourselves as his holy priests.

As living stones and holy priests, serving God in his spiritual temple, we offer to him a spiritual sacrifice. This spiritual sacrifice negates the need for the many sacrifices and offerings we read about in the Old Testament.

We are living stones built into a spiritual temple, being prepared for a holy priesthood to offer spiritual sacrifices.

This thinking is so countercultural to the way most Christians live today that it is hard for many to consider, let alone embrace. Yet through Jesus we are called to do things in a new way.

This truth can change everything—and it should.

How can we better live our lives as living stones, built into a spiritual house? How can our actions better reflect the knowledge that our bodies are temples?

[Discover more about our bodies as temples in 1 Corinthians 6:19–20.]

DAY 11: A ROYAL PRIESTHOOD
1 PETER 2:9–10

But you are a chosen people, a royal priesthood, a holy nation, God's special possession, that you may declare the praises of him who called you out of darkness into his wonderful light.
(1 Peter 2:9)

In this verse, Peter describes us in four ways: as a chosen people, a royal priesthood, a holy nation, and God's special possession.

We've already discussed us being the elect, his chosen people, in "Day 1: Living in Exile" and "Day 2: Chosen." We'll touch on being a holy nation in a bit, and we can read more about being his possession in Ephesians 1:13–15.

First, let's focus on the idea of priesthood.

In the Old Testament, only select people can be priests. Priests must be a descendant of Aaron (a small part of the tribe of Levi) and be male. This automatically rules out most of the tribe of Levi and all the other eleven tribes, as well as all women.

This is quite restrictive. As a result, a few are in, and most are out.

Jesus changes all of this. In Jesus's church, the door to priesthood flies wide open. We're all eligible to be priests. In fact, we are all priests by virtue of being his followers.

Under Jesus, the priesthood as a special ordained position becomes obsolete. Instead, the priesthood becomes normal, something we all should embrace as our calling. As priests, we minister to each other and shouldn't expect someone else to do the job for us.

The priesthood of believers says that as followers of Jesus, we are all priests—every one of us. Let's discover what this means.

Though the Bible never mentions the phrase *priesthood of believers*, we find the idea of us all being priests in both the Old and New Testaments.

Peter says that as we come to Jesus, the living Stone, we will likewise become living stones, built into a spiritual house, to be a royal priesthood, offering spiritual sacrifices to Father God. We talked about this in "Day 10: Living Stones."

As today's text says, this makes us a chosen people, a royal priesthood, and a holy nation.

This idea of being a royal priesthood, a holy nation (of priests), however, doesn't start with Peter. It goes back to Moses. It was God's desire for his people to become a kingdom of priests and a holy nation (Exodus 19:5–6).

God wanted to speak to his people directly (Exodus 19:9). But they were afraid of hearing God talk to them. Instead, they asked Moses to be their go-between (Exodus 20:18–19).

It's only after the people reject God's plan for them to be a kingdom of priests and for him to speak to them directly that he institutes the office of priest. It seems that having designated priests is a contingency plan.

Though we see priests throughout the Old Testament, we never see the nation of Israel or Judah emerge as a country filled with priests.

Through Jesus, this changes in the New Testament—at least it should. Through our Savior, we are God's chosen people, a royal priesthood, and a holy nation. We are, at last, God's nation of priests.

What must we change to better function as part of a royal priesthood? What can we do today to be a priest to someone else?

[Discover more about us being priests in Revelation 1:6.]

DAY 12: LIVE GOOD LIVES
1 PETER 2:11–12

Live such good lives among the pagans that, though they accuse you of doing wrong, they may see your good deeds and glorify God on the day he visits us. (1 Peter 2:12)

Today's passage opens with two words we've already encountered in Peter's letter: foreigners (1 Peter 1:17) and exiles (1 Peter 1:1). Instead of being insulted by Peter referring to us as foreigners and exiles, we should embrace it as the reality of who we are.

As followers of Jesus, we don't belong here. We're just passing through on our journey to the eternal home that awaits us in heaven. Our real domicile is not in this world.

With this perspective, we realize we're here for the short-term. With eyes fixed on Jesus, we maintain our earthly status as foreigners and exiles, both in a physical sense and with a faith-filled, future-focused, spiritual expectation.

We are indeed foreigners, but do we act like it?

Living as foreigners means we have a different focus, different goals, and different priorities than the people around us. And people should see that difference.

The point is, we don't fit in here—or at least we shouldn't. We're outsiders subsisting in a society that doesn't understand our thinking or our way of life. We live in a culture opposed to Jesus.

Peter doesn't tell his audience then—or us now —to adapt and settle down. Instead, he says to abstain from sinful desires. Though we are called to be holy like God (Leviticus 19:2) and work out our salvation by how we live (Philippians 2:12–13), Peter doesn't mention either of these two reasons.

Instead, he gives us a different goal.

Peter wants our lives to stand as a powerful example among those who don't believe, that is, the pagans. Though they may oppose us—and even accuse us of doing wrong—the good lives we live and the good deeds we do should be evident to them all. The result of this will be them giving glory to God. (Peter will again touch on the subject in 1 Peter 3:15–16.)

We see this idea of standing out for our faith practices brilliantly shown in the life of Daniel. King Darius appoints 120 satraps—that is, rulers or princes—to be over the provinces. A trio of administrators oversee the satraps. Daniel is one of the three. He distinguishes himself among them all, so the king plans to promote him over the entire kingdom.

But the other administrators and satraps don't like this plan. They want to get rid of Daniel, but they can find no corruption in him or grounds to charge him (Daniel 6:1–4).

May the same be true with us, just as Peter teaches.

Do we live our lives to blend in or to stand out for Jesus? Will our enemies be unable to find any fault in our conduct?

[Discover more about how we live in Daniel 6:4, Matthew 5:16, 2 Corinthians 8:21, and James 3:13.]

DAY 13: SUBMIT TO AUTHORITY
1 PETER 2:13–14

Submit yourselves for the Lord's sake to every human authority: whether to the emperor, as the supreme authority, or to governors. (1 Peter 2:13–14)

Today's passage opens with the word *submit*. It's not a word we like to hear today. No one wants to submit, yet Peter tells us to do so. In fact, *submit* is a recurring word in his letter, appearing in five verses—more times than any other book in the Bible.

It's clear that Peter wants us to submit to others as we follow Jesus. Yet these acts of submission are not to debase us but to result in bringing glory to God.

Peter's first instruction to submit is in reference to every human authority. The specific examples he gives are the emperor (that is, the head of state) and governors (those appointed by the emperor).

We do this for God's sake.

Though some nations today still have an emperor as their supreme authority, others have a prime minister, president, chairman, premier, chancellor, monarch, or director. Some function as dictators, even though they have a different title.

Regardless of their title or what we may think about our leaders, we must submit to their authority, just as Peter told his audience to submit to the emperor.

By extension, we must likewise submit to those appointed to serve under our nation's supreme authority. This can include governors, law enforcement, and the judiciary.

Peter doesn't say that we are to submit to them if they are good leaders or we agree with them. When he tells us to submit, he gives us no conditions. This suggests that we're to submit to them whether they are good rulers or evil ones.

In Paul's letter to the Romans, he tells them to be subject to governing authorities, for God has established them all. Rebelling against the authorities is rebelling against what God has instituted. We obey them to avoid punishment and keep a clear conscience. We are even to pay the taxes we owe (Romans 13:1–7).

David also shows respect for the supreme human authority in his life, even though King Saul is intent on killing him. David refuses to kill his enemy when he can do so, acknowledging that Saul is the Lord's anointed (1 Samuel 24:6).

Though this command to submit is unconditional, it's not absolute. When Peter and John are commanded to stop telling other people about Jesus, Peter replies, "We must obey God and not people" (Acts 5:28–30).

From this we see a principle that we must obey every human authority unless it contradicts what God tells us to do. Our Lord is our ultimate authority, and we must always obey him.

In what areas can we do better at submitting to every human authority? When should we obey God instead of human rulers?

[Discover more about respecting authority in 1 Timothy 2:1–4.]

DAY 14: SHOW PROPER RESPECT
1 PETER 2:15–17

Show proper respect to everyone, love the family of believers, fear God, honor the emperor. (1 Peter 2:17)

The reason Peter tells us to submit to every human authority is so that we'll do what's right, what's good. It's God's will for us that by doing good, we'll silence the ignorant talk of foolish people. That is, through our actions, others will have no grounds to criticize us or, by extension, to criticize our Lord. This is the will of God.

Peter continues and says that—despite being under the rule of human authority—we are to live as free people. That is, not under the law or bound by rules. We must take care, however, not to use this freedom in Jesus as a cover for evil living, that is, as an excuse to sin (Romans 6:1–2). Instead, we are to live as God's slaves.

As we do this, we should show everyone respect, love other Christians, fear God, and honor human authority.

The first element of Peter's fourfold instruction is to show everyone respect. This doesn't mean just the people who respect us or the people who believe as we do. It means everyone.

This includes those who disagree with us or even oppose us. We need to show them respect, that is, to esteem them and honor them, to show appreciation and defer to them. Given the context of the prior verses, this especially applies to those in human authority over us.

Next, Peter tells us to love the family of believers. This means all who follow Jesus, even if they hold different theological views than we do, align with a different church or denomination, or worship and serve God in different ways. Loving them goes beyond respect. Love stands as the highest form of relating to them (1 Corinthians 13:13).

Third, we are to fear God. Jesus has already said that we are to love God (Matthew 22:37). Now we see a need to fear God too. This is a respectful fear. (See "Day 7: Live in Reverent Fear.")

Just as it would be wrong to love God and not fear him, we would be equally in error if we fear him but don't love him. We must do both. We must balance our love of the Almighty with a reverent fear of who he is and what he can do (Luke 12:5).

Fourth is the command to honor the emperor. We covered the emperor in yesterday's reading. Then our action was to submit to him. Now we add to it the requirement to honor him as well.

The instruction to honor builds upon the instruction to submit. We must do both.

How well do we do at both loving God and fearing him? How can we best show honor to authority when we submit to them?

[Discover more about respect in Romans 13:7 and 1 Thessalonians 4:11–12.]

DAY 15: BE A GOOD EMPLOYEE
1 PETER 2:18–21

Slaves, in reverent fear of God submit yourselves to your masters, not only to those who are good and considerate, but also to those who are harsh. (1 Peter 2:18)

The second of Peter's five verses about the need to submit relates to slaves. Most of us reading these words today are not slaves. Does this mean the passage doesn't apply to us? Maybe. Maybe not.

The idea of slavery in biblical times is likely different from how we perceive it today. Consider Joseph in the Old Testament. He spends many years as a slave, first in Potiphar's household and later in prison (Genesis 39).

As Potiphar's slave, Joseph oversees his master's household, having the authority to do what he feels is in his master's best interest. Though he doesn't have the freedom to leave without repercussions, he faces few constraints in his work for his master.

Later, Joseph lands in prison. Though remaining a prisoner—and lacking the freedom to leave—he rises to a position of authority. The warden puts him in charge of the prison and makes him responsible for all that happens there.

Though Joseph is technically a slave in both situations, he has much authority and the latitude to act within the confines of his situation. Though not all slaves would fare as well as Joseph, this gives us a glimpse into what ancient slavery could have looked like and how it was far different from how we envision it today.

In the Old Testament law, Moses addresses the proper way to deal with slaves. He even talks about what to do with a servant who loves his master and doesn't want to leave (Exodus 21:5–6).

From this perspective, it's not too much of a stretch to extend Peter's instructions to slaves to apply to us today as employees. Likewise, we can extend the instructions to masters to apply to employers.

As an employee, we should do what our employer tells us to do. Not only is this the best way to stay employed and earn a living, but it also honors God.

Yet this principle of obeying our employers doesn't just apply to those who treat us well. It also applies to those employers who are harsher. God commends us when we bear up under their unjust treatment. Jesus's suffering for us provides an example for us to follow.

Paul also teaches on this, telling us to obey our earthly masters just as we would obey Jesus. We are to work well when they're watching and even when they're not. We should serve our employers whole-heartedly, as if serving God (Ephesians 6:5–9).

How well do we do at submitting to our employers? How have we responded when our employers treated us harshly?

[Discover more about slavery in Romans 6:15–23.]

DAY 16: FOLLOW THE SHEPHERD
1 PETER 2:22–25

For "you were like sheep going astray," but now you have returned to the Shepherd and Overseer of your souls. (1 Peter 2:25)

Yesterday's reading ended with the idea that Jesus's suffering for us can serve as an example when we suffer for him. Peter continues that theme by explaining how the sinless Jesus suffered for us when he died on the cross for our sins. He did this as an example for us to follow.

Peter likens Jesus to a shepherd caring for his flock. We were sheep going astray, wandering to and fro. But now we have turned to Jesus, our

Shepherd and our Overseer. As our Shepherd and Overseer, he will take care of us.

Though sheep may appear as lovable animals, they're not too intelligent. They wander away. They get into trouble. And they're quite helpless to get out of the messes they get into. They need help if they are to survive.

In this way, we are sheep. We aren't too intelligent, we wander away, and we get into trouble. We need our shepherd to rescue us from our messes. We need Jesus.

This idea of Jesus being our shepherd first occurs in the Old Testament. Jeremiah quotes the Lord as saying that he will not run away from being our shepherd (Jeremiah 17:16). He will not flee when danger comes. He will stand firm and protect us. We can depend on him as our shepherd.

Ezekiel likewise quotes God as saying that he will look after his sheep just as a trustworthy shepherd will look after the animals under his care. God, as our shepherd, will rescue us from all the places we wander (Ezekiel 34:12). He will give us one shepherd, through David, who will tend to us (Ezekiel 34:23).

Speaking of David, he declares the Lord is his

shepherd, and therefore, he lacks nothing (Psalm 23:1). Matthew later writes that God will send his people someone to shepherd them (Matthew 2:6). We see this confirmed in John's future-focused vision. He writes that the Lamb—that is, Jesus—will sit on the throne and be the people's shepherd. He'll lead them to living water and wipe away their tears (Revelation 7:17).

John writes extensively about Jesus being our good shepherd. He will protect us, even die for us. We will follow him, and he will keep us safe (John 10:1–18).

Though John is the only writer in Scripture to refer to Jesus as our good shepherd, the writers of Hebrews call him a great Shepherd. Though we may not be as familiar with this label, this elevates Jesus from being good to great—a great Shepherd. (Hebrews 13:20–21).

Last, we see that Peter will later use the adverb *chief* to describe Jesus as their shepherd. When Jesus comes again, he'll appear as our Chief Shepherd (1 Peter 5:4).

How should we react to the idea that we are sheep and often need help? What do we think of Jesus being our Good Shepherd, Great Shepherd, and Chief Shepherd?

[Discover more about sheep in Matthew 9:36, Mark 14:27, and Luke 15:3–7.]

DAY 17: WIN THEM OVER
1 PETER 3:1–6

Wives, in the same way submit yourselves to your own husbands so that, if any of them do not believe the word, they may be won over without words by the behavior of their wives. (1 Peter 3:1)

The third of Peter's five verses about the need to submit relates to wives, which occurs in today's passage. I've always felt it unfair to tell wives to submit to their husbands without telling guys the same thing. Yet let's look back to the curse Adam and Eve receive when they disobey God.

To the woman, God says, "You will desire your husband, but he will rule over you" (Genesis 3:16).

Because of the curse brought about by sin, husbands will rule over their wives. Therefore, Peter instructs wives to submit to their husbands.

But the reason for their submission isn't to make them subservient. It's to win over unbelieving husbands. They do this without saying a thing and through their character.

What are these characteristics? They are purity, reverence, and the inner beauty of a gentle and quiet spirit. Let's look at these four traits.

To be pure is to be innocent and chaste. Purity is the absence of spiritual or moral defilement. This looms as a lofty standard in our world today, where few are pure. Instead, society pushes the limits of proper behavior, abolishes moral boundaries, and celebrates impurity. This should not be the case for the God-honoring wife—or for any of us as God's children.

The second trait is living a life of reverence. Reverence is being in awe, showing respect, and acting in love. Should we direct this reverence to God or to husbands? It's not clear from the text, but let's start with reverence to God. I suspect reverence toward husbands may automatically follow.

Third, we read to be gentle. We understand gentleness as considerate, kind, amiable, and tender.

Gentle is not to be harsh. Just as wives should be gentle toward their husbands, we should all be gentle toward each other.

Last is the trait of a quiet spirit. Of the four characteristics, a quiet spirit stands as the most difficult one to explain. Consider it as having a peaceful countenance, to possess an inner calmness. Though our world today dismisses those with a quiet spirit, it's a trait worthy of us pursuing to honor God.

As wives do these four things, they point their husbands to Jesus. For the unbelieving spouse, this can move him to a point of following Jesus. Yet for the believing husband, wives who embody these traits can affirm him on his faith journey and encourage him to follow Jesus more fully.

When this happens, the entire family receives blessings, and God receives honor.

How well does our behavior point others to Jesus? Whether married or not, what needs to change in our relationships to those closest to us?

[Discover what Paul says about wives submitting in Ephesians 5:22–24 and Colossians 3:18.]

DAY 18: CONSIDERATE AND RESPECTFUL

1 PETER 3:7

Husbands, in the same way be considerate as you live with your wives, and treat them with respect. (1 Peter 3:7)

Peter has just addressed wives and told them to submit to their husbands so that they may win them over. We covered this in yesterday's reading. Now Peter turns his attention to husbands. In the same way wives are to submit to their husbands, husbands are to be considerate in their interactions with their wives and respect them.

This also ties back to sin entering the world when Adam and Eve disobeyed God's one rule. They ate from the forbidden tree and received punishment.

The punishment was banishment from their idyllic paradise and a series of curses. One curse brought about by sin was that Adam would rule over Eve (Genesis 3:16). This sin-produced curse extends to all marriages today. In a generic sense, men rule over women. This is the result of sin.

For sin's curse to specify husbands ruling over their wives, things would have been different before. This suggests that in God's created order, Adam didn't rule over Eve, and Eve didn't need to submit to Adam. Given this, it's easy to see Adam and Eve coexisting in Eden as equals. We can see this as God's original plan.

Yet because of sin, wives need to submit to their husbands, and husbands need to be considerate and respectful of their wives.

For husbands to be considerate of their wives is to show regard for their spouses' needs and feelings, to be kind. Being considerate is marked by being deliberate and intentional with their interactions. It's showing care.

Shouldn't we all be considerate with each other?

James writes that one of the several admirable traits flowing from wisdom is being considerate (James 3:17). In short, showing consideration results from wisdom.

In Paul's letter to his protégé Titus, he lists being considerate as a characteristic to remind the people to pursue (Titus 3:1–2). By extension, we can receive this as an instruction for us today. First, we should remind people to be considerate. Second, we should model this ourselves and be considerate of others.

Next, husbands are to treat their wives with respect. We covered respect in "Day 14: Show Proper Respect." Respect is to regard someone with honor or esteem. It's showing appreciation and even deferring to them.

In this way, husbands are to respect their wives.

The reason Peter tells wives to submit to their husbands is to win them to Jesus. The reason Peter tells husbands to be considerate of their wives and treat them with respect is so that nothing will hinder their prayers.

This doesn't imply that God will always say yes to husbands' prayers if they're considerate and respectful toward their wives. But it does say that failing to offer consideration will hinder the prayers of husbands.

Whether we're married or not, we should be considerate of others and treat them with respect.

What should we do if we feel our prayers are hindered? How can we show others consideration and respect?

[Discover what Paul says about husbands in Ephesians 5:25–32 and Colossians 3:19.]

BONUS CONTENT: THE WEAKER PARTNER

Treat them with respect as the weaker partner. (1 Peter 3:7)

I squirm a bit when Peter talks about women as the weaker partner. This verse specifically addresses husbands and wives. It's part of a longer passage about marriage. Yet it offends my sensibilities because I strive to view men and women as equals.

In looking at multiple versions of this verse, some say *weaker partner,* and many use the phrase *weaker vessel.* Some verses clarify that this weakness refers to physical characteristics, which we can accept because biologically men are stronger than women.

The Message version of the Bible says, "as women they lack some of your advantages" (1 Peter 3:7, MSG).

The Expanded Bible clarifies this even further, using the phrase as "the less empowered one" and explains that in that society women had less power and authority (1 Peter 3:7, EXB).

Can we properly expand our understanding of this teaching to go beyond marriage and produce a general principle?

If we extend Peter's instructions beyond marriage, everyone (both men and women) should take care in how we treat others—both female and male—who may be a *weaker vessel* to us: those who lack our advantages, who aren't as empowered, and who possess less authority.

As we do so we promote a God-honoring justice (2 Corinthians 7:11).

What do we need to do to respect those who are weaker than us? What should we do if we see ourselves as the weaker vessel?

[Discover more about being weak in 1 Corinthians 12:22 and 2 Corinthians 12:10. Read about speaking up for others in Proverbs 31:8–9.]

DAY 19: LIVE IN HARMONY
1 PETER 3:8–12

Finally, all of you, be like-minded, be sympathetic, love one another, be compassionate and humble. (1 Peter 3:8)

Peter opens this passage with the word *finally*. This suggests he's wrapping up his letter, but he's not. He's only halfway through. Instead, he's wrapping up this part of his teaching, which is about how husbands and wives should treat each other.

Peter writes, "all of you." Given the context, all of you applies to both husbands and wives, to all married people. Yet we won't go wrong to extend *all of you* to encompass everyone, whether married or not.

In this, Peter gives us five traits to emulate.

First, we should be like-minded. That means to be of one accord, to agree with each other. This is a challenging command, especially given the divisive world we live in today. Yet just because it's hard doesn't mean we don't have to pursue it.

Paul likewise tells the Church of Philippi to be like-minded, having the same love, and being one in spirit and mind. This is because we are united in Jesus (Philippians 2:1–2).

Next, Peter tells us to be sympathetic. Interestingly, this is the only passage in the Bible that tells us to be sympathetic. Yet this doesn't mean we don't need to take it seriously.

To be sympathetic is to be favorably inclined toward others, to be agreeable and congenial. Just as with being like-minded, our world today has an overall lack of sympathy. As followers of Jesus, we need to change that.

Third, Peter tells us to love one another. This is the most repeated "one another" command in the Bible. Peter has already mentioned it in 1 Peter 1:22. Paul also writes this in Romans 13:8. And John often says to love one another, most notably in 1 John 4:7–11.

Most importantly, Jesus tells us to love one

another (John 13:34–35). The teacher also tells us that after the greatest command to love God, we should love our neighbor as much as we love ourselves (Matthew 22:37–39).

Fourth on Peter's list of key traits is to be compassionate. To show compassion is to have sympathy for others who are in sorrow or struggling with pain. This goes beyond merely being empathetic. Compassion results in an appropriate response. In Ephesians, Paul likewise says to be kind and compassionate to one another (Ephesians 4:32).

Last is to be humble. Humility is marked by modesty in how we think and act. It's the opposite of arrogance and pride. Humility is not a characteristic that today's world respects. But God's perspective is different.

Jesus says that he is humble (Matthew 11:29). May we be humble as he was humble. Jesus also teaches that those who try to exalt themselves will be humbled and the humbled will be exalted (Luke 14:11).

Peter will later write to clothe ourselves in humility and that God will lift the humble in due time (1 Peter 5:5–7).

Which of these five God-honoring traits do we need to work on the most? What can we do to start today?

[Discover Peter's other instructions of how we're to treat one another in 1 Peter 1:22, 1 Peter 4:9, 1 Peter 5:5, and 1 Peter 5:14.]

DAY 20: DO GOOD
1 PETER 3:13–14

Even if you should suffer for what is right, you are blessed.
(1 Peter 3:14)

Peter opens today's passage with a rhetorical question: "Who's going to harm you if you do what is good?" While common sense tells us that no one will, we know that in our upside-down world, we could be attacked when we do good. We too often are.

Our world often celebrates what God opposes and opposes what God commands. Though this seems like a recent development, it's not.

Isaiah saw this many centuries ago. He proclaimed woe on those who call evil good and good evil, who mistake darkness for light and bitter for sweet (Isaiah 5:20). The world had it backward then, just as people have it backward now.

Given this, it shouldn't surprise us when people criticize us for doing good, even though it seems illogical. When we follow Jesus and obey him, we should expect opposition. That's why Jesus tells us to discern what we'll have to give up, to count what it will cost us to follow him (Luke 14:25–35).

Is this a reason to shy away from doing good things for our Lord? Of course not! We should obey him regardless of what other people say or think. God—and God alone—is our judge. His opinion is the only one that really matters.

Even if we suffer for doing what is right, we should take comfort in knowing that God will bless us, regardless. Peter will later build on this when he says that we're better to suffer for doing what is good than for doing evil (1 Peter 3:17).

In several of his letters, Paul likewise tells his audience to do good (Galatians 6:10, Ephesians 2:10, and 1 Timothy 6:18). The writers of Hebrews also teach this (Hebrews 13:16).

Jesus teaches extensively about doing good (Luke 6:27–36). He says we're to love our enemies and do good to those who hate us. We are to bless those who curse us. We are to pray for those who mistreat us. If we're attacked, we're to turn the other cheek. We should do to others what we want them to do to us.

Besides loving our enemies, we need to do good to them, to treat them right. We should even lend without expecting them to pay us back.

When we do these things, our reward will be great. We'll be blessed.

When have we failed to do good for fear of what other people might say or do? How can we better love our enemies and pray for them?

[Discover more about blessings in Matthew 5:1–10 and Luke 6:20–24.]

DAY 21: PREPARED TO ANSWER
1 PETER 3:15–17

Always be prepared to give an answer to everyone who asks you to give the reason for the hope that you have. (1 Peter 3:15)

Peter says to be prepared—that is, to be ready—to give an answer when someone asks about our faith. If we're to make the most of these opportunities, we must be alert and look for them. (See "Day 6: Be Alert.")

The context for this instruction is in doing good, which we covered in yesterday's reading. The bookends for this *do good* passage are 1 Peter 3:13 and 1 Peter 3:17.

As we do good, we'll get people's attention. Yes,

sometimes the attention we garner is negative, but most of the time, the attention is positive. People see the good things we do. They want to know why. They're curious.

As we do good—with no motivation other than to serve and for no reward—others see an unexplainable hope within us. It's such a foreign concept to many that we stand out. They want to know why.

This presents the easiest opportunity for us to tell people about Jesus. We let our actions open the door for us. Then people ask us to explain. They're a receptive audience and ready to hear what we have to say. This is when we tell them about Jesus.

But we need to prepare for this opportunity when it occurs. And if we're doing good, opportunities will arise. The only question is when.

Here are four ideas of how to be prepared to give a ready answer.

First, we immerse ourselves in God's Word. The more we hide God's Word in our heart (see Psalm 119:11), the more likely it is to flow out of our mouth when we have the opportunity to talk about Jesus. In this way, we begin each day focusing on God's Word. Then his words go with us throughout the day.

Second, we rely on the Holy Spirit to give us the

right words to say. Jesus even encourages us to do so (Luke 12:11–12). Though the situation is a bit different, he tells his disciples to not be concerned about what they'll say when they're questioned by rulers and authorities. Instead, they're to depend on the Holy Spirit to give them the right words at the right time.

A third way to be prepared is to practice. When I have important words to say, I plan them. I practice them. If practicing is your preferred way to be prepared, then go for it.

A final thought about how to be prepared is to pray. Not only should we pray beforehand that God will give us the right words to say, but we can also make a brief petition to our Lord at the moment someone asks about our faith. Equally important is to pray for the opportunities to make a response.

In doing these four things, we'll be prepared to give an answer to everyone who asks the reason for our hope.

Which of these four tips most resonates with us? Are we praying for opportunities to tell others about Jesus?

[Discover more about being prepared in Psalm 85:13 and 2 Timothy 4:2.]

DAY 22: ALIVE IN THE SPIRIT
1 PETER 3:18–19

For Christ also suffered once for sins, the righteous for the unrighteous, to bring you to God. He was put to death in the body but made alive in the Spirit. (1 Peter 3:18)

Today's passage is one of the most concise and yet richest explanations in the Bible about salvation through Jesus. We will do well to study it, internalize it, and use it to shape our understanding of who Jesus is and what he did for us.

This verse—and our salvation—starts with Christ, which means Messiah. Jesus is the Messiah. That is, Jesus is the Christ, which people often shorten to Jesus Christ or sometimes simply Christ.

Without Christ as our Messiah, we couldn't receive our salvation. It all hinges on him and not ourselves. We only need to receive—through faith —what he did for us (Romans 10:10 and Hebrews 10:39).

Jesus suffered once—and only once—for all our sins. This is unlike the Old Testament sacrifices, which repeated annually to atone for the sins the people committed that year. Then they had to do it again the next year: year after year, over and over.

Jesus's sacrifice is a once-for-all ransom of us. In his singular sacrifice—during which he received and carried the punishment for all our wrongs—he died for all the sins, of all people, through all time. He died to cover our past mistakes and our future blunders, the ones we haven't yet made. Besides our own sins, he died for all the sins of those who've gone before us and for all the sins of those who will follow us.

Jesus is sinless. He is righteous. We are not. We are sinful. On our own, we are unrighteous. Yet the righteous Jesus died for his unrighteous creation. The righteous for the unrighteous. The sinless for the sinner. Jesus for us—for you and for me.

In dying for us, Jesus does so to bring us to Father God through him. In this way, we are reconciled to Papa. Jesus is the only way to the Father (John 14:6). There are no other paths to salvation.

When Jesus died on the cross as the ultimate sacrifice to end all sacrifices, his body suffered death, but this wasn't the end. Even though the physical part of him died, the spiritual part of him did not. His physical death makes him spiritually alive—again.

He becomes spiritually alive just as he was before he came to earth as a baby to save us, and just as he is today waiting for us to join him when our physical bodies die (John 14:1–3). Then we, too, will be alive in the Spirit.

What part of this verse do we appreciate the most? How can we best thank Jesus for saving us?

[Discover more about salvation in Ephesians 2:8–9.]

DAY 23: BAPTISM
1 PETER 3:20–22

This water symbolizes baptism that now saves you also—not the removal of dirt from the body but the pledge of a clear conscience toward God. (1 Peter 3:21)

Baptism is a New Testament word. It never appears in the Old Testament. The practice of baptism starts with John the Baptizer when he baptizes people for the repentance of their sins (Mark 1:4).

Baptism continues with Jesus, through his disciples (John 4:1–3). He baptizes us with the Holy Spirit and fire (Luke 3:16). Baptism extends to his followers—then and now—through the baptism of the Holy Spirit (Acts 2:1–4). We practice water baptism today to show this symbolically (Acts 2:38).

Some Bible teachers connect New Testament baptism with the Old Testament ceremonial washing of the priests. Yet Peter connects baptism with Noah and the flood. Here's what happened.

God sees that the world is corrupt and wants to make a clean start with humanity. He will begin again with Noah and his family. This includes Noah and his wife, their three sons, and their three daughters-in-law. That's eight people in all. God tells Noah to build a huge boat and prepare for a coming flood, even though there's no evidence to suggest it would happen (Genesis 6:9–22).

It takes Noah and his family one hundred years to build the ark as the Lord commanded. Then God sends some animals in pairs, two by two, to Noah. Noah and his family board the ark, along with all the animals God sent. God shuts the door to the ark and seals them in. They are safe. The rain begins. It rains and rains. It's a deluge. The Earth floods. All the people outside of the ark drown (Genesis 7).

It's a sad day of judgment for them because of their sins. Yet Noah and his family survive. They are safe in the ark (Genesis 8). These eight people live.

God tells Noah to be fruitful and increase in number (Genesis 9:1). This repeats what God said earlier to Adam and Eve.

It's humanity's do-over. It's creation 2.0. The human race begins again through Noah and his family. The rest of the Bible is about them and their descendants.

Just as the ark saved Noah and his family from the death that surrounded them, baptism symbolically shows our salvation, of us being saved from the death that surrounds us.

God saved Noah through the ark. This foreshadows baptism. God saves us through Jesus's death. We see this symbolically portrayed in baptism.

Baptism is a ceremonial cleansing, but not one to remove dirt from our body. Instead, it's the pledge—the response—of a clear conscious toward God. This is because, through Jesus, our sins are forgiven. As a result, we can, therefore, approach Father God with a clear conscience.

He remembers our sins no more (Hebrews 8:12 and Hebrews 10:17).

What do we think about Peter connecting the flood with baptism? What does our baptism mean to us today?

[Discover more about baptism in Romans 6:3–4, 1 Corinthians 12:13, Galatians 3:26–27, and Ephesians 4:4–6.]

DAY 24: LIVE FOR GOD
1 PETER 4:1–5

As a result, they do not live the rest of their earthly lives for evil human desires, but rather for the will of God. (1 Peter 4:2)

Today's passage about suffering opens with the word *therefore*. This reminds us to consider the words that precede this transitional term so that we may best understand what follows.

As covered in yesterday's reading, the prior text is about baptism. How does baptism connect with suffering?

Baptism is a symbolic reminder of us aligning with Jesus for our salvation. He provides us with salvation because he physically suffered and died for our sins.

Because the perfect Jesus suffered in his body when he died for imperfect us, we will likewise suffer in our body because we are done with sin—that is, we are dead to sin. As a result, we no longer live earthly lives. We've moved past the carnal to focus on the spiritual.

This means that we live spiritual lives for the will of God. We live not for ourselves but for him. We leave the past behind and no longer do what we once did. Though nonbelievers—the pagans—persist in these behaviors, we do not.

What is this list of past behaviors? It's debauchery, lust, drunkenness, orgies, carousing, and idolatry. Though we may push past this list with a smug satisfaction that none of them apply to us, we should consider all that these words entail.

Debauchery is an extreme indulgence in sensual pleasures. We normally think of this being sexual, but it can refer to any sensual indulgence. This could include too much eating or drinking.

Next is lust. Lust is a longing for something we don't have. Again, we normally attribute sexual connotations to this word. But we can also lust for power, money, and possessions. We covet what others have. When coveting possessions, it's materialism. Materialism is a rampant form of lust today.

Third, we have drunkenness. We may think of drunkenness as habitual inebriation, but it also refers to a single instance of intoxication. Therefore, anyone cognitively impaired commits drunkenness.

The fourth item on our list is orgies. This relates to unrestrained indulgence, usually sexual activity and drinking. Yet a shopping spree is also an orgy of spending. Overeating is an orgy of food.

Next is carousing. It's consuming large amounts of alcohol, often accompanied by boisterous activity and merrymaking. Doesn't that make a pub crawl a modern form of carousing?

Sixth, we have idolatry. In a literal sense, idolatry is worshiping idols. In practice, idolatry is an excessive devotion to something. Today's most common form of idolatry is worshiping self. When we habitually elevate our needs over the needs of others, we're giving excessive devotion to ourselves. It's being self-centered and worshiping the idol of self.

As followers of Jesus, we're called to suffer in our body, just as he exemplified suffering in his. When we do so, we push into our past all forms of debauchery, lust, drunkenness, orgies, carousing, and idolatry.

The result is being in the will of God.

Given our expanded understanding of these six words, which ones do we need to more fully push into our past? How is this the will of God?

[Discover more about the will of God in Hebrews 10:36 and 1 John 2:17.]

DAY 25: CONFUSING VERSES
1 PETER 4:6

For this is the reason the gospel was preached even to those who are now dead. (1 Peter 4:6)

When we encounter a passage in the Bible we don't understand the tendency is to rush past it to get to the next part. We hope those words will make more sense. So is the case with this verse. We'd like to skip it and move on to the next verse about the end times.

Yet a better response is to pause. It's an opportunity for us to consider the words in the hope of gaining new insight into the text.

When I strive to do this, I implore the Holy

Spirit to give me supernatural insight. Sometimes this happens right away, while other times I must persist, waiting days and even years to receive clarity. For other verses, I'm still waiting.

Such is the case for this one. It's confounding at best.

How do we comprehend the idea of preaching the gospel to those who are now dead? For Bible commentators brave enough to offer their opinion, they give multiple plausible explanations with less-than-clear conclusions. Even more perplexing is a lack of consensus among them.

Occam's razor—also called the principle of parsimony—tells us that the simplest explanation is usually the correct one.

So rather than debating about the meaning of the word dead, who this refers to, and what era it covers, let's assume that somehow people who are dead can still hear the gospel. This somehow allows for their judgment by human standards and for them to receive spiritual life.

Don't be concerned if this still makes little sense. That's okay. Embrace it as a delightful mystery of God's omniscient, omnipotent, and omnipresent power. His knowledge is infinite; ours is finite. There are some things we'll never understand.

Here's another confusing passage.

The reading for "Day 20: Alive in the Spirit" skipped another perplexing verse. The text says that after being made alive, Jesus went to make proclamation to the imprisoned spirits (1 Peter 3:19).

Who are imprisoned? Where are they being held? Does *spirit* refer to the spirit part of each person, as in body, soul, and spirit (1 Thessalonians 5:23)? Or might *spirit* imply angels or other supernatural beings?

My bigger question is wondering if these two verses connect. Will Jesus somehow preach to the spirits of those who are dead and imprisoned?

I don't know. I doubt anyone does.

What I know is that in John's epic end-time vision, which we read in the book of Revelation, God gives people multiple chances to repent. Even when it seems like they've run out of time, he still gives them an opportunity to turn to him.

Peter has already written that our patient God doesn't want anyone to perish. Instead, he wants everyone to come to repentance (2 Peter 3:9).

The key is that we should turn to him today while we have the chance (Isaiah 55:6). Now is the time to receive God's favor and is the day of salvation (2 Corinthians 6:2).

How content are we in not understanding everything about God and the Bible? Though it starts with salvation, what are we putting off for tomorrow that we should do today?

[Discover more about us and God in Job 40:1–2.]

DAY 26: END-TIME INSTRUCTIONS
1 PETER 4:7–11

The end of all things is near. Therefore be alert and of sober mind so that you may pray. (1 Peter 4:7)

Peter writes that the end is near. This was the perspective of many people two thousand years ago. They expected Jesus could return at any time. Though he didn't, most of his followers have persisted in this perspective for the last two millennia. Today, many people are convinced we're living in the end times, that the end of all things is near.

Given this, we should keep the tension of the timing of his return in balance, simultaneously expecting Jesus's return at any moment, while planning a life lived with intention for his glory until the day we die.

With this perspective, we must focus on what matters most.

Peter's first item is to be alert and sober-minded. Alertness means being watchful and attentive. It requires focus. At a base level, to be sober-minded means to avoid intoxication. In a more general sense, sober-minded is to hold every thought captive (2 Corinthians 10:5). This allows us to focus on godly things.

The reason for being alert and sober-minded is so that we may pray. If we're not focused or thinking clearly, we'll struggle in our prayers.

Next is love. In "Day 19: Live in Harmony" we discussed the importance of loving one another. Peter writes that love covers many of our shortcomings, that is, a multitude of sins. We need to make love a priority. Through Paul we see love as our highest calling (1 Corinthians 13:13).

Third is hospitality. To offer hospitality to one another in a God-honoring way we must do so gladly and without grumbling. Not only are we to be gracious hosts to our guests, but when we are guests, we must strive to be easy to serve and not cause our hosts to grumble.

Next, Peter tells us to use our gifts to serve others. We must be faithful stewards of the abilities God has graciously given us. Each one of us has different abilities; we are not the same. We must focus on our own giftedness and not the gifts of others (1 Corinthians 12).

Peter's next two items give us examples of using specific gifts.

Consider those who speak. In the context of giftedness, this applies primarily to apostles, prophets, and teachers. But it's also a lesson for us all (Matthew 12:36–37). We must choose the words we say with care, as if speaking the very words of God.

The second example is those who serve. We should not serve in our own strength, but in God's. In doing so, God will receive the praise through Jesus. To him belongs all the glory.

How should we understand Peter's warning that the end is near? Which of these actions might we want to give more attention to?

[Discover more about God's gifts to us in Romans 12:6–8, 1 Corinthians 12:8–10, 1 Corinthians 12:28, and Ephesians 4:11–13.]

DAY 27: REJOICE IN SUFFERING
1 PETER 4:12–19

However, if you suffer as a Christian, do not be ashamed,
but praise God that you bear that name. (1 Peter 4:16)

The word *Christian* occurs in Scripture but not often. Not counting the subheadings that were later added, *Christian* only appears three times in Scripture.

Luke uses *Christian* twice in the book of Acts. He says the word first popped up in Antioch (Acts 11:26). It was a label given to those who follow Jesus, the Christ. The intent of those who coined this word, however, may have been to disparage Jesus's followers, using it to mock their devotion.

Later, King Agrippa uses the word *Christian* when talking to Paul at his trial (Acts 26:28).

Peter is the only other biblical writer who uses the word *Christian*. He writes about Christians—that is, followers of Jesus—who suffer for their faith. He encourages them to not be ashamed but to praise God.

Putting God first and following Jesus as his disciple will probably result in us facing difficulties. We may encounter ridicule, we may suffer embarrassment, and we may be attacked, either verbally or physically. We should expect to suffer when we put Jesus first. This may be in small ways or big ways, but we will suffer.

This should not come as a surprise. Jesus says so. That's why he tells people to first consider the cost before following him (Luke 14:25–33).

Yet Jesus also proclaims blessings on us when we're persecuted for our faith (Matthew 5:11–12). Our response to those who persecute us should be to love and pray for them (Matthew 5:44), be good to them (Luke 6:27–28), and help them (Romans 12:20).

Though we will face trouble in the world, as Jesus's followers we should be encouraged because he has overcome the world (John 16:33) and nothing can separate us from him (Romans 8:35).

In our suffering, Peter continues by saying we must take care that we suffer for Jesus and not because of our own shortcomings, such as being a murderer, thief, criminal, or even a meddler. In an earlier passage, he says it's better to suffer for doing good than evil (1 Peter 3:17).

Peter concludes this passage by saying that when we suffer according to God's will, we should focus on two things: The first is to commit ourselves to our faithful Creator. The second is to continue to do good.

When our walk with Jesus aligns closely with him, we will face hardship. This persecution, in effect, confirms our faith. Although unwanted, this opposition becomes a praiseworthy event.

May we praise our Heavenly Father when we undergo persecution for Jesus.

How ready are we to suffer for Jesus? What should we think if we're not persecuted for following him?

[Discover more about persecution in 2 Corinthians 12:10, Hebrews 12:7, and 1 Peter 5:10.]

BONUS CONTENT: MORE ABOUT SUFFERING

But rejoice inasmuch as you participate in the sufferings of Christ, so that you may be overjoyed when his glory is revealed. (1 Peter 4:13)

A recurring theme in Peter's first letter to Jesus's church is suffering. The word occurs in nineteen verses, some of which we've already covered.

Here is a list of passages in 1 Peter about suffering.

- 1 Peter 1:6
- 1 Peter 1:11

- 1 Peter 2:19–23 (See "Day 15: Be a Good Employee")
- 1 Peter 3:8
- 1 Peter 3:14–18
- 1 Peter 4:1 (See "Day 24: Live for God")
- 1 Peter 4:12–19 (See "Day 27: Rejoice in Suffering")
- 1 Peter 5:1
- 1 Peter 5:9–10 (See "Day 31: Beware the Roaring Lion")

What do these passages teach us about suffering? How should we react when we suffer for Jesus?

[Discover more about suffering in Romans 8:17–18, 2 Thessalonians 1:5, and James 5:10.]

DAY 28: A CROWN OF GLORY
1 PETER 5:1–4

When the Chief Shepherd appears, you will receive the crown of glory that will never fade away. (1 **Peter** 5:4)

P eter writes his next passage to elders. Identifying himself as one, he addresses his fellow elders. Though we could think of this as being the office of elder, which some churches have, we're better off to apply it to all church leaders and our spiritual mentors. This can include ministers and pastors.

Those who aren't church elders may rush past this passage, viewing it as not applicable. But don't. There are three reasons everyone should consider these words.

First, Peter tells spiritual leaders how to act and the proper attitudes they should have. Second, it guides us as we choose our spiritual leaders. Third, it provides general insight that applies to anyone in a leadership position, as well as to all followers of Jesus.

Paul writes about the qualifications of church leaders (1 Timothy 3:1–10 and Titus 1:6–9). Over the years, I've seen churches refer to these passages when making their selections.

What I've not seen is churches referring to Peter's teaching on the subject. But what he has to say is more important. Peter doesn't focus on leader qualifications. He focuses on leader actions. In doing so he gives us five characteristics that mark a God-honoring elder.

First, they are to serve as shepherds of Jesus's sheep. They're to watch over the flock as overseers. This shouldn't be out of obligation but should stem from a willingness to be a shepherd.

Next, they should not seek dishonest gain. They shouldn't use their position to manipulate people for their own financial benefit. This isn't to imply that pastors shouldn't be compensated or can't be well paid. But money shouldn't be their primary motivator.

Third, they should be eager to serve. A church leader who isn't excited about their role shouldn't be in that position.

Next, they shouldn't lord their position of authority over their charges. Though we will do well to honor our spiritual leaders, they would be wrong to demand it. They shouldn't take pride in their position in the church, including their title.

Last, they should serve as examples to those under their care. They should exemplify Jesus.

When they do these five things, they will receive a crown of glory from Jesus, the Chief Shepherd, when he returns.

In the same way, we can all hope that Jesus will give us a crown of glory for what we have done throughout our lives to serve him and advance his kingdom.

How can these five characteristics of elders inform what we do? Whether or not we receive a crown from Jesus, what are we doing for him?

[Discover what Paul says about being an example in 1 Corinthians 11:1.]

DAY 29: YOUNG PEOPLE
1 PETER 5:5

In the same way, you who are younger, submit yourselves to your elders. (1 Peter 5:5)

To day's passage is the fifth verse in Peter's concise letter that tells us to submit.

We've covered *submit* in "Day 13: Submit to Authority," "Day 14: Show Proper Respect," "Day 15: Be a Good Employee," and "Day 17: Win Them Over."

Looking at this verse in isolation, it tells young people to submit to their elders, that is, the people who are older than them. Not only is this a sign of respect to our elders, but it also acknowledges that they have—or at least they should have—more life experience and knowledge than we do, which we can benefit from. When we submit to them, we benefit from their wisdom.

Some specific groups of elders that we should submit to are parents, teachers, and employers. We should also submit to our church and spiritual leaders, as well as governmental authorities and law enforcement officers.

As we covered in Day 13, these commands to submit are unconditional but not absolute. When the religious leaders command the disciples to stop talking about Jesus, Peter replies, "We must obey God and not you" (Acts 5:28–30). Therefore, we must obey every human authority unless it contradicts what God tells us to do.

This means we must obey elders, unless they go against what the Bible says. It's important to remember this exception. In the past, too many people—including those in church leadership positions—have abused their authority.

We should never allow others to tell us to do something that God tells us not to do.

This is a good generic understanding of this verse. But the context tells us that elder is not generically anyone who is older than us, but specifically our church leaders. We get this from the transitional phrase *in the same way*. This means to consider the context of Peter's prior teaching.

Here, our elders specifically relate to those who are our spiritual overseers: ministers, pastors, elders, deacons, teachers, and the like. We must submit to them.

Yet we must condition this with the caveat that we first submit to God and his Word. If the two stand in disagreement, we submit to God and disregard what our religious elders tell us to do.

In what ways can we apply this verse in a general sense to those who are older than us? When submitting to our spiritual leaders, how can we best balance what they tell us to do with what the Bible says?

[Discover more about submitting in Romans 13:5, 1 Corinthians 16:15–16, Ephesians 5:21–27, Hebrews 12:9, and Hebrews 13:17. Read the five verses where Peter tells us to submit in 1 Peter 2:13, 1 Peter 2:18, 1 Peter 3:1, 1 Peter 3:5, and 1 Peter 5:5.]

BONUS CONTENT: PETER REFERENCES THE OLD TESTAMENT

God opposes the proud but shows favor to the humble.
(1 Peter 5:5)

Though there's nothing in the Bible to indicate that Peter had received advanced religious training, he expertly weaves Scripture into his letters.

Here are the verses where Peter brings Old Testament Scripture into his teaching:

- 1 Peter 1:16 quotes Leviticus 11:44–45 and Leviticus 19:2
- 1 Peter 1:24–25 quotes from Isaiah 40:6–8

- 1 Peter 2:6 quotes Isaiah 28:16
- 1 Peter 2:7 quotes Psalm 118:22
- 1 Peter 2:8 quotes Isaiah 8:14
- 1 Peter 2:22 quotes Isaiah 53:9
- 1 Peter 2:25 quotes from Isaiah 53:4–6
- 1 Peter 3:10–12 quotes Psalm 34:12–16
- 1 Peter 3:14 quotes Isaiah 8:12
- 1 Peter 4:18 quotes from Proverbs 11:31
- 1 Peter 5:5 quotes Proverbs 3:34
- 2 Peter 2:22 quotes Proverbs 26:11

We can see from this that Peter knew the Scriptures well and communicated it with ease. Since it's unlikely he had these various texts to refer to, he had committed these passages to memory.

In addition, 2 Peter 1:17 quotes the spoken words of God, as witnessed by Peter and recorded in Matthew 17:5, Mark 9:7, and Luke 9:35

May we follow Peter's example in knowing and referencing the Bible.

With no resources to consult, how well would we do to recall Scripture? What can we do to be more ready to share the truth about God's Word with others?

[Discover more about the importance of knowing what the Bible says in Psalm 119:11.]

DAY 30: BE LIFTED UP
1 PETER 5:6–7

Humble yourselves, therefore, under God's mighty hand, that he may lift you up in due time. (1 Peter 5:6)

The idea of humility is not popular in today's culture. Our society does not celebrate the humble. In fact, it does the opposite. Today's world commends those who promote themselves: the proud, the self-congratulatory, and the self-promoters. It even applauds those who carry themselves with a smug arrogance.

Yet our Lord's perspective is different. Peter tells us we should humble ourselves under God's power, that is, under his mighty hand.

The passage from yesterday's reading ended

with a call to humility. Peter encourages us to clothe ourselves with humility toward one another. This is because God opposes the proud and shows favor to the humble (Proverbs 3:34 and Matthew 23:12).

To clothe ourselves with humility is a visual reminder to put on humility, to wear it just as we wear clothes. When we do this, humility goes everywhere we go. Just as we'd never leave home without clothes, we must never go anywhere without humility. It's that important.

By implication, there's never a time to not be humble. We should keep pride at bay.

Humility should be our posture to others.

Yet there's more. Today's verse carries the insightful word *therefore*. This clues us in to looking at the prior passage as we consider the current one.

Just as we humble ourselves before others, we should likewise humble ourselves before God, under his mighty hand.

Jesus viewed himself as being humble (Matthew 11:29). The four biographies of Jesus confirm this. Though it may seem haughty for someone to declare themselves as humble, when it's true, it's not prideful. It's reality.

Jesus later says that for those who exult themselves—that is, the prideful—they will face humility.

The opposite is also true. Those who humble themselves—that is, who place others ahead of themselves—will be exalted.

Peter explains how we will be exalted. He says that God will lift us up in due time. Though we're left to wonder when due time will occur, we can count on the promise that God will one day lift the humble. Due time may occur during our life, or it may occur in heaven after we die. Perhaps it's both.

Though our world today doesn't celebrate the humble, God's perspective is the opposite. He promises to lift the humble, and that's what matters. What he thinks is more important than what people think.

In this way, we will be lifted.

What do we think about the idea of being humble? When has our pride kept us from being humble like Jesus?

[Discover more about being humble in Ephesians 4:2, Philippians 2:8, James 1:9–10, and James 4:6–10.]

DAY 31: BEWARE THE ROARING LION
1 PETER 5:8–14

Be alert and of sober mind. Your enemy the devil prowls around like a roaring lion looking for someone to devour.
(1 Peter 5:8)

P eter opens today's passage with the instruction to be alert and of sober mind. Does this sound familiar? This is the third time he gives us these two commands.

The first time he tells us to keep our mind alert and our bodies fully sober is so we can focus on Jesus (1 Peter 1:13). The second time Peter tells us to be alert and of sober mind is so that we may pray, because the end is near (1 Peter 4:7).

Now the disciple mentions this duo a third time. Be alert. Be of sober mind.

To be alert means to be on the lookout, to watch out for danger. To be of sober mind means to not get drunk. By extension, it's to not be impaired in any way.

We must be alert and sober because an enemy lurks among us. The devil is on the prowl. We are the prey.

Since we can't see the devil in our physical world, Peter gives us an image we can understand. Peter likens the devil to a roaring lion. This lion is on the hunt, looking for supper. The lion wants to devour us. So too with the devil.

If a lion were about, we'd certainly be on high alert and stay sober-minded. We'd focus on being safe and avoiding the peril that lurks in the shadows. Yet the unseen danger of the devil poses a greater threat. This is why we must be alert and sober.

Peter's prescription for dealing with the devil is to resist him.

James gives us the same advice. He says to resist the devil, and he will flee from us (James 4:7). Though James doesn't tell us how to resist the devil, Peter does. He says we are to stand firm in our faith.

From a practical standpoint, there are three ways to stand firm in our faith. One is to seek God in prayer. A second is to immerse ourselves in God's Word, specifically focusing on his many promises. A third is to not struggle alone (Ecclesiastes 4:12). That is, we should be in a spiritual community with like-minded believers.

As we do so, we should know that others in our faith family are undergoing the same types of suffering as we are. By implication, the devil wants us to suffer. Though we may not avoid all suffering, we can certainly minimize it by being alert and sober-minded.

Thankfully, because of God's grace, our suffering will not last long. After we have suffered for a while, our Lord will restore us and make us strong, firm, and steadfast.

What can we do to be alert and of sober mind? How can we better resist the devil?

[Discover more about resisting in Hebrews 12:4.]

BONUS CONTENT: A SUPPORTIVE TRIO

With the help of Silas, whom I regard as a faithful brother, I have written to you briefly, encouraging you and testifying that this is the true grace of God. (1 Peter 5:12)

P eter ends his letter by mentioning three people.

First is Silas. Silas helped Peter with his letter. Perhaps Peter doesn't know how to write, and Silas takes dictation. This is likely the same Silas whom Paul mentors in the book of Acts (Acts 15:39–40). Silas is now with Peter and helps him with his letter.

Next up is "she who is in Babylon." We don't

know who this cryptic phrase refers to, with the speculation diverging widely. What we know is that she is chosen, just like Peter's audience. Therefore, she is one of them. She sends her greetings.

Last, Peter mentions Mark, whom he identifies as his son. We know Peter is married, but Scripture doesn't mention any offspring. Mark could be a biological son. Alternately, Mark could be a spiritual son, just as Paul views Timothy (1 Timothy 1:2).

If Mark is a spiritual son to Peter, it could be a reference to John Mark. Sometimes Scripture refers to him as Mark, sometimes as John, and other times as "John, also called Mark" (Acts 12:25). Many people speculate that he's the author of the book of Mark.

These three people are with Peter as he writes this letter. Silas helps him with the composition, while the unidentified woman and Mark chime in to send their greetings. They may have also provided input into the contents.

They all have a part in Peter's letter to Jesus's church.

Who can we help as they encourage others in their faith?
Who can we come alongside to provide ministry support?

[Discover more about John Mark in Acts 12:12, Acts 13:5, Acts 13:13, Acts 15:37–40, 2 Timothy 4:11, and Colossians 4:10.]

2 PETER

As with 1 Peter, 2 Peter is written by Jesus's disciple. Though it is not immediately apparent, the audience of this letter is the same as for his first one (2 Peter 3:1). Therefore, it's Peter's second letter to Jesus's church. Like his first one, 2 Peter universally applies to all Christians everywhere.

The key topics in 2 Peter encourage us to continue to grow in our faith, strive to avoid false teaching (heresy), and to finish strong as we look forward to spending eternity with Jesus.

Peter also knows he will soon die. He wants to do all he can to make sure we remember his teachings about Jesus after he's gone. The most direct way is through his letter. But his wording is vague, leading us to wonder if he expects to also somehow be able to help us remember once he's in heaven (2 Peter 1:12–15).

Regardless of what he means in this verse, his letter stands as his legacy. It contains his last words to us, almost like his last will and testament. This isn't to ensure Peter's place in history but as a final lasting effort to teach, guide, and encourage the followers of Jesus before the disciple dies.

Peter also mentions Paul's writing in his letter. This means the prolific apostle has already penned multiple epistles, and Peter knows of their content. He admits Paul says some things that are hard to understand (2 Peter 3:15–16).

Though this may seem like a dig, we may better receive it as an acknowledgment that Paul's writing is more intellectual, while Peter's is simpler, more suited to everyday people. Even so, Peter also writes of some things that are hard to understand.

But with the Holy Spirit's guidance we can better understand these difficult passages from both writers.

*What should we do now to encourage future generations—
starting with our family and friends—to keep their focus on
Jesus? What legacy can we leave?*

[Discover more about finishing strong in Acts 20:24,
Hebrews 12:1, and 2 Timothy 4:7.]

DAY 32: EVERYTHING WE NEED
2 PETER 1:1–4

[Jesus's] divine power has given us everything we need for a godly life through our knowledge of him who called us by his own glory and goodness. (2 Peter 1:3)

One of God's characteristics is his omnipotence; he is all powerful. As part of the Trinity, Jesus is therefore omnipotent. Through his divine power, he gives us everything we need. Though some people may stop reading the passage at this point, don't do that.

Jesus doesn't give us everything we need, period. Jesus gives us everything we need to live a godly life.

But why should we want to live a godly life?

We don't live a godly life to earn our salvation,

get God's attention, or garner his favor. We don't live a godly life to cause him to love us more, make our life easy, or receive his esteem.

Instead, we live a godly life in response to what God has done for us through Jesus. Jesus died for the wrong things we have done—and will do—to make us right with Father God. In this way, Jesus reconciles us with Papa.

This is why we want to live a godly life. It's our way of saying "thank you" to Jesus for our salvation and for our right standing because of what he did for us when he died on the cross.

Jesus is our example of living a godly life. It's our knowledge of him that shows us what living a godly life looks like. This starts with doing what he did. The books of Matthew, Mark, Luke, and John detail this for us. In this way, these four biographies of Jesus are a great place to inform us in how to live a godly life for him.

Yet, Paul warns us that anyone who strives to live a godly life in Jesus will face persecution (2 Timothy 3:12–13).

While this truth may discourage us from wanting to live a godly life, that doesn't mean we should give up on it or not even try. When we align ourselves with Jesus and follow him as a disciple, we are to pick up our cross and follow him (Luke 9:23 and Luke 14:27). This means that suffering and persecution could result.

When we follow Jesus as his disciple, this is more than an intellectual ascent. In following him, we do so through our actions. We live a godly life.

What are we doing to live a godly life? What outcome do we expect when we follow Jesus into godly living?

[Discover more about persecution in Romans 8:35, 2 Corinthians 12:10, and Hebrews 10:33.]

DAY 33: ADD TO YOUR FAITH
2 PETER 1:5–9

For this very reason, make every effort to add to your faith goodness; and to goodness, knowledge; and to knowledge . . .
(2 Peter 1:5–6)

For the very reason of our salvation through Jesus—and living a godly life for him—Peter gives us a progressive list of eight traits to pursue, with each one flowing from the other. It starts with faith and culminates in love.

First is faith. By faith, we accept the gift of salvation through Jesus and follow him. Faith is believing in what we cannot see (Hebrews 11:1). After faith comes goodness.

Goodness is the state of being good. The dictionary explains that it's to be generous and offer kindness. Goodness is the outgrowth of our faith; it's faith in action. (See Ephesians 5:8–10 and James 2:24–26.) After goodness comes knowledge.

Our knowledge of Jesus grows as we know him more fully. We become familiar with him, are aware of who he is, and better understand him. (Consider Luke 8:10.) It's the mental part of our relationship with him. From our knowledge stems self-control.

Self-control is a personal discipline to do what is right and not do what is wrong. (See Titus 2:1–14.) As we live a life of self-control, we persevere.

Perseverance is to keep going when we face difficulties. We don't stop. We don't give up. We press forward. (See James 1:2–4.) Then we add godliness to our perseverance.

Godliness is being like God. Though we will never achieve complete godliness, we can move in that direction. (See 1 Timothy 4:8.) From godliness springs mutual affection.

Mutual affection is a reciprocal appreciation of other followers of Jesus. We don't look down on others, nor do we consider them better than us. Instead, we journey through life together for Jesus. (Consider Romans 12:10.) An outgrowth of mutual affection is love.

Love isn't a feeling but an attitude that produces action (1 Corinthians 13:1–7). We are called to love God and love others (Mark 12:29–31). It's that simple.

When we possess these eight qualities—faith, goodness, knowledge, self-control, perseverance, godliness, mutual affection, and love—and increasingly grow in them, the result will keep us from being ineffective and unproductive for Jesus.

Instead, they will move us toward greater effectiveness and increased productivity in advancing the kingdom of God.

But if we lack these eight qualities, we are near-sighted and even blind. We have forgotten that Jesus has forgiven our sins. May that never be.

Which of these qualities would we like to see more of in our lives? In what ways can we be more effective and productive for Jesus?

[Discover more about being unproductive in Titus 3:14.]

DAY 34: MAKE EVERY EFFORT
2 PETER 1:10–15

Therefore, my brothers and sisters, make every effort to confirm your calling and election. (2 Peter 1:10)

Today's passage opens with the delightful word *therefore*. To best understand what follows this word, we must first look at what precedes it. The prior part of Peter's letter talks about our faith in Jesus and his divine power and nature. This motivates those who follow him to live a life that possesses eight key qualities. (See "Day 33: Add to Your Faith".)

Because of this truth, we are to make every effort to confirm our calling and election.

Our calling results from God's invitation to us to

follow Jesus—of him calling us into salvation. We answer his call when we say yes to Jesus, make a U-turn with our lives, and become his disciples.

Our election is a bit harder to understand. It's not like we ran for public office and were elected. We can better understand our election by looking at the secondary meaning of the word, which means being chosen or selected. In a spiritual sense, this refers to God choosing us. He picked us! We are his choice. He appointed us to receive salvation through Jesus.

Despite this, we need to make every effort to confirm God's calling and election of us. This starts with our faith in Jesus's saving sacrifice. As we covered in yesterday's reading, we build on our faith with goodness, knowledge, self-control, persever-ance, godliness, and mutual affection, capping everything off with love.

Peter says that when we do these things, we will never stumble. This doesn't mean our life will proceed with a perfect, no-problem bliss. It simply means that when we encounter bumps on our journey down life's pathway, we will not fall.

This is the present result of confirming our calling and election. The future part of confirming our election and calling will occur later when we go to heaven.

When we arrive there, we'll receive a rich welcome, granting us access into the eternal kingdom—the everlasting realm—of Jesus Christ, who is our Lord and our Savior.

Not only does our calling and election make a difference in our lives here on earth, but it also ushers us into heaven to enjoy everlasting life with our Creator.

Peter wants us to be sure that we remember this, even after he is gone. It's that important.

How do we react to the idea of being called and elected? Are we making every effort to confirm it?

[Discover more about our election in Romans 9:11–12 and Romans 11:25–29.]

DAY 35: GOD'S TESTIMONY OF JESUS
2 PETER 1:16–21

He received honor and glory from God the Father when the voice came to him from the Majestic Glory, saying, "This is my Son, whom I love; with him I am well pleased."
(2 Peter 1:17)

Peter reminds his audience that the good news he shared with them about Jesus wasn't something he made up. It wasn't some cute or clever story about something that didn't happen. It was real.

He and the other disciples were there to witness it personally. Peter has a firsthand account of all that Jesus did. That is what he shared.

Specifically, Peter talks now about an event we

call the transfiguration. James and John are there, too, joining Peter to witness Jesus's supernatural transformation.

All four ascend a mountain. Suddenly Jesus's face shines; it's glorified. His countenance transfigures. His appearance changes.

Even more unexpected, Moses and Elijah—though long dead—appear too. They talk with Jesus.

Peter wants to commemorate this unprecedented event. He suggests building them each a shrine or tabernacle in their honor. Before Jesus says anything, a bright cloud covers them.

The voice of Father God comes from the cloud. "This is my Son," he says. "I love him and am pleased with him. Listen to what he says" (Matthew 17:5).

In one succinct declaration, God validates Jesus as his Son, affirms Jesus's ministry, and commands the disciples to listen to him.

Peter confirms that he—along with James and John—was with Jesus when this happened and heard Father God's words. This is God's testimony about Jesus. Now it's Peter's testimony too.

But there's more.

Besides the spoken words of God, we have the

written words of God. We can read about them in Scripture. These came as prophetic messages from the prophets as inspired by the Holy Spirit.

True prophecy, Peter reminds us, doesn't come from a prophet's own opinion, will, or understanding. Prophecy isn't the product of human determination. Instead, God's prophets are conduits of his words, as delivered to them by the Holy Spirit. They write what he says to share with the people, both then and now.

In this way, Father God tells us about Jesus through his spoken word and through his written Word.

How can we be encouraged knowing that Peter—the writer of this letter—was an eyewitness to what Jesus did and said? What do we think about the prophecies in the Old Testament that foretell about Jesus?

[Discover more about Jesus's supernatural transfiguration in Matthew 17:1–13, Mark 9:2–13, and Luke 9:28–36.]

DAY 36: BEWARE OF FALSE PROPHETS
2 PETER 2:1–22

But there were also false prophets among the people, just as there will be false teachers among you. (2 Peter 2:1)

Peter warns that just as there were false prophets in the Old Testament Scriptures, his audience had false teachers among them too. The same is true for us today.

We must be on the lookout for them. Here's what Peter says we should watch out for.

First, they teach destructive heresies.

A heresy is anything that runs counter to what the Bible teaches. A destructive heresy is even worse. It discredits the foundation of our faith. A key example is Jesus dying for our sins and rising from the dead to save us. This is a pillar of our faith. Without Jesus's redemptive work, our beliefs don't matter.

Yet we must be careful when we use the word *heresy*. A heretic opposes what the Bible teaches. Some proclaim ideas that aren't in the Bible, which their followers accept as truth. This is heresy. We must oppose it. It's not heresy, however, if we merely disagree with them over their interpretation of Scripture.

Second, with greedy intent, these false teachers exploit their listeners with fabricated stories. They just make things up and proclaim it as truth. Instead, we should be like the Berean Jews, who checked the Scriptures to make sure that what Paul said was true (Acts 17:11).

Furthermore, these false teachers blaspheme—decry and speak against—what they don't understand. Even if they do this out of ignorance or laziness, it's no excuse. Sadly, I've heard ministers do this today. Instead, they should take care to proclaim only what is true.

Peter continues by saying these false teachers carouse in broad daylight. They tarnish our celebrations. Jude concurs (Jude 1:12–13). These false teachers have adulterous eyes and don't cease from sinning. They seduce the unstable and are full of greed.

They have wandered from the straight path toward Jesus and followed the error of Balaam (Numbers 22–24, Jude 1:11, and Revelation 2:14). Balaam's mistake was placing worldly profit over God-honoring obedience.

Just as Peter wants us to be on the alert for these teachers, he also warns that they'll be paid back for the harm they have caused Jesus's church and his followers. Though Peter doesn't share the extent of their punishment, it should surely give us pause to make certain we avoid their error. We shouldn't even listen to them.

How should we react to these warnings against false teachers? How can we be more like the Bereans and study the Bible so we can recognize heresy?

[Discover more about false prophets in Isaiah 44:24–26, Jeremiah 14:14, Lamentations 2:14, Ezekiel 13:9, Hosea 11:6, and Matthew 7:15.]

BONUS CONTENT: IF-THEN

If this is so, then the Lord knows how to rescue the godly from trials and to hold the unrighteous for punishment on the day of judgment. (2 Peter 2:9)

In 2 Peter 2:4–9, we read four *if* statements. The passage ends with a concluding *then* proclamation to encourage and comfort us. The conclusion is that God will rescue the godly and punish the unrighteous on the day of judgment.

These four *if* statements that lead into this conclusion all reference Old Testament events. Here are the passages for further study.

1. The angels who sinned: Genesis 6:1–4, with support in Jude 1:6.
2. The ancient world that sinned: Genesis 6:5–8:19, with support from Hebrews 11:7 and 1 Peter 3:20.
3. Sodom and Gomorrah: Genesis 19:12–29, with support in Matthew 10:15, Matthew 11:23–24, and Jude 1:7.
4. Lot: Genesis 19:18–21, with support from Deuteronomy 2:19 and Luke 17:28–30.

If God did these four things, then he will surely rescue those who follow him. We can count on it.

How can knowing that God will rescue us from trials encourage us in our daily living? What do we think about the unrighteous being punished on the day of judgment?

[Discover more about the day of judgment in Matthew 12:36 and 1 John 4:17.]

DAY 37: WHOLESOME THINKING
2 PETER 3:1–2

Dear friends, this is now my second letter to you. I have written both of them as reminders to stimulate you to wholesome thinking. (2 Peter 3:1)

P eter states that his letters are to stimulate us to wholesome thinking. This isn't one more instruction for us to pursue. Instead, it's an acknowledgment that all the contents in both his letters will stimulate wholesome thinking in us.

Interestingly, this phrase *wholesome thinking* doesn't appear anywhere else in the Bible, so we can't use Scripture to help us interpret Scripture this time. Yet we can understand wholesome thinking as that which promotes moral well-being, to produce spiritual health in us. We are to steer our thoughts in that direction.

Paul writes we are to pursue whatever is excellent and praiseworthy, thinking about those things. This includes whatever is true, noble, right, pure, lovely, and admirable (Philippians 4:8). This list of six traits gives us a great place to start for wholesome thinking.

In another of his letters, Paul says to capture every thought and make it subject to Jesus. We should fight against all ideas contrary to God. We do this when we take every thought captive and force it to submit to Jesus (2 Corinthians 10:5).

Likewise, Solomon instructs us to guard our hearts and everything that flows through them (Proverbs 4:23). This includes our thoughts.

The direct way Peter expects us to stimulate wholesome thinking is to read his two letters. By extension, all of Scripture can likewise stimulate wholesome thinking.

Prayer is another way to turn our attention from the things of this world—unwholesome thinking—to the things of God, which is wholesome thinking.

The world bombards us with distractions to turn us away from wholesome thinking. Today's news, entertainment, and social media all threaten to fill us with negativity, with unwholesome think-ing. We must resist their influence, which we can rightly see as coming from our enemy, the devil. He does not want us to cultivate wholesome thinking. He promotes the opposite.

As we covered in "Day 31: Beware the Roaring Lion," James tells us to "Resist the devil and he will flee from you" (James 4:7).

We can do this by fixing our eyes on Jesus (Hebrews 3:1). We should focus on him and him alone. This will best allow us to focus on what is wholesome.

How well do we do at stimulating wholesome thinking? In what ways has unwholesome thinking gotten us into trouble?

[Discover more about wholesome thinking in Colossians 3:2–10.]

DAY 38: THE LAST DAYS
2 PETER 3:3–9

*Above all, you must understand that in the last days scoffers
will come, scoffing and following their own evil desires.*
(2 Peter 3:3)

Peter warns us that in the last days, people
will scoff at the idea that the world is
about to end. Instead, they'll follow the
evil desires of their hearts. Implicitly, they'll mock
God's words and dismiss what he says, not believing
that the end is near. Rejecting the Creator, they'll
pursue their own sinful impulses.

In "Day 26: End-Time Instructions," we
covered that we should maintain a balance over the

tension of the timing of his return, simultaneously expecting it at any moment, while planning a full life lived for him should he tarry.

Yet we should trust God's words and his promises.

Peter calls our attention to God's creation, which came into being when he spoke. By his power, the water he created later flooded the world and destroyed humanity. By his word, he further says our present realities will likewise one day be destroyed by fire.

This will result in judgment and destruction for those who don't follow him. He did this once during the time of Noah, and he'll do it again in our future. We just don't know when. But we shouldn't assume that because it hasn't happened yet, it isn't going to. It will occur. We can count on it.

To help us better comprehend our Lord's perspective of time as we wait for the last days to occur, recall that God exists outside of the space-time reality he created. As a result, time—as we perceive it—isn't a factor to him. Just as he exists outside of our world and peers in, he exists outside of time and peers in too.

Peter reminds us that from our perspective, a

day to God is like a thousand years to us. In the same manner, a thousand years are like a day (Psalm 90:4).

Though we've already waited two thousand years, we shouldn't accuse God of being slow at keeping his promises. Instead, the delay shows his patience (also see 2 Peter 3:15). His desire is for no one to perish in their unbelief. Rather, God's wish is for everyone to come to repentance, for them to turn from their sins to follow Jesus and be reconciled with him.

We shouldn't, however, assume this means everyone will enjoy an eternal reward in heaven. Though God wants us there, he doesn't mandate it. He won't force us to join him. Each person he created has the free will to decide their eternal fate. Yet to give them more time to turn to him, God delays the last days.

Even so, the end draws nearer. We must be ready.

How should we react when we encounter those who scoff at God's word? What do we think of the idea that God doesn't want any of his children to perish?

[Discover more about the last days in Isaiah 2:2, Micah 4:1, 2 Timothy 3:1, and Hebrews 1:1–3.]

DAY 39: A NEW HEAVEN AND A NEW EARTH

2 PETER 3:10–13

But in keeping with his promise we are looking forward to a new heaven and a new earth, where righteousness dwells.
(2 Peter 3:13)

Right after telling us that God is delaying his judgment to give people more time to repent, Peter says that the end—that is, the day of the Lord—will come unexpectedly. It'll be like a thief coming to rob us; it will happen when we least expect it.

This aligns with Jesus's teaching. He says if the homeowner had known when the thief was coming in the middle of the night to steal from him, he'd have kept watch and protected his home (Matthew 24:43). Just as a homeowner doesn't know when he'll be robbed, we don't know when Jesus will return to usher in the end of time.

Paul likewise confirms that we don't know when the end will occur. He also uses the thief-in-the-night imagery. People will think they're safe, but destruction will happen in an instant. He then alludes to the labor pains of pregnant women. Both labor and the end will happen suddenly. There's no escape from either (1 Thessalonians 5:1–3).

In his teaching about the end times, Jesus references Noah. Noah builds his giant boat to save his family and select animals from the impending deluge that will destroy everything else. Yet the people happily go about their lives, not aware they will soon drown (Matthew 24:36–39 and Luke 17:26–27).

Jesus also reminds us about Lot. God plans to destroy Sodom for its wickedness. The people are blissfully unaware that destruction awaits them. Instead, they go about their daily lives. They eat and drink. They buy and sell. And they plant and build. The day angels drag Lot away from the city, destruction rains upon the town and kills its people (Luke 17:28–30).

Since everything will likewise one day be destroyed, Peter challenges us in the lives we'll live as this day approaches. Though we could live sinful lives like the unbelievers around us, we ought to instead live holy and godly lives. This is the best way to be ready when the Lord comes again.

When this occurs, fire will destroy the heavens —our sky and outer space. The immense heat will melt it.

We should not, however, despair over its destruction. Just as God promised, he will provide a new heaven and a new earth for his followers to live in.

Besides Peter, both Isaiah and John prophesy that this will occur (Isaiah 65:17 and Revelation 21:1).

In this way, we should not fear the end of time and the destruction that will occur. Instead, we can embrace this as the moment when we will see the complete fulfillment of us spending eternity with God.

Do we look at the end of time with fear or anticipation? As we await our reward, how can we best live holy and godly lives?

[Discover what Jesus says about the end times in Matthew 24:3–51, Mark 13:5–37, and Luke 21:5–36.]

DAY 40: MAKE EVERY EFFORT
2 PETER 3:14–18

So then, dear friends, since you are looking forward to this,
make every effort to be found spotless, blameless and at peace
with him. (2 Peter 3:14)

Because we're looking forward to spending eternity with God in a new heaven and a new earth, Peter tells us to do three things. We don't do these, however, to get God's attention, garner his favor, or earn salvation. We've already received these three things. Instead, Peter's instructions are a response to what we already have.

First, Peter tells us to make every effort to be found spotless, that is, sinless. We are to sanctify ourselves. As we covered in "Day 8: Purified

Through Obedience," we are already *positionally* sanctified. This happened the moment we decided to follow Jesus. Yet, our bodies are still moving in that direction to become *progressively* sanctified. This is what Peter is telling us to move toward as we await Jesus's return.

Next, Peter tells us to make every effort to be found blameless. We could view this as a repeat of being found spotless before God. But we can also look at this as encouragement to be found blameless before others. If we live a life without blame, we give others no opportunity to besmirch the name of our Savior through our bad behaviors.

Third, Peter tells us to make every effort to be at peace with Jesus. Usually when we think of living at peace, it's with other people. Yet to live at peace with Jesus reminds us to remove anything from our behavior or thinking that might cause frustration or tension toward him.

At this point in Peter's conclusion to his letter, he points out Paul's more intellectual writing style. Some of what Paul says is hard to understand, and some people distort his words. In fact, they do this with all of Scripture, which will result in their own destruction. They are both ignorant and unstable.

Since Peter has warned us, we, therefore, must

be on guard to not fall victim to the same thing. We don't want to get carried away by misinterpretations of Scripture. If we do, we may fall away from our secure position in Jesus. This isn't a threat that God will take away our salvation. Jesus's promise to us is guaranteed. He will not take it back. Yet, just as we chose to follow Jesus, we could also choose to walk away. Though our position is secure from Jesus's standpoint, we have free will and can turn from him. May that never be.

As a prescription, Peter tells us to grow in grace. A simple definition of grace is to receive good things that we don't deserve. Our salvation through Jesus is a prime example of his grace. We don't deserve it, but he gives it to us anyway. His unconditional love is another example of his boundless grace. We also see his grace in many other ways.

The second of Peter's recommendations is to grow in the knowledge of Jesus Christ. We covered this in "Day 32: Everything We Need." As we understand Jesus more fully, we protect ourselves from the possibility of turning our backs on him.

As we grow in the grace and knowledge of Jesus, we do so for his glory. This glory occurs both now in our present world and later in heaven.

Amen.

What can we do to make every effort to be found spotless, blameless, and at peace with Jesus? How can we better grow in the grace and knowledge of our Savior?

[Discover more about God's grace in John 1:17, Acts 15:11, Romans 3:22–24, 1 Corinthians 1:4, and 2 Timothy 1:9.]

If you liked *1 and 2 Peter Bible Study,* please leave a review online. Your review will help others discover this book and encourage them to read it too.

Thank you.

BOOKS IN THE 40-DAY BIBLE STUDY SERIES

Which book do you want to read next in the 40-Day Bible Study Series?

- Dear Theophilus (the Gospel of **Luke**, formerly That You May Know)
- Dear Theophilus, **Acts** (formerly Tongues of Fire)
- Dear Theophilus, **Isaiah** (formerly For Unto Us)
- Dear Theophilus, **Minor Prophets** (formerly Return to Me)
- Dear Theophilus, **Job** (formerly I Hope in Him)
- Living Water (**John**)
- Love Is Patient (**1 and 2 Corinthians**)

- Revelation Bible Study (formerly A New Heaven and a New Earth)
- Love One Another (**1, 2, and 3 John**)
- Run with Perseverance (**Hebrews**)
- James and Jude Bible Study
- Matthew Bible Study

FOR SMALL GROUPS, SUNDAY SCHOOL, AND CLASSES

1 and 2 Peter Bible Study makes an ideal eight-week Bible study discussion guide for small groups, Sunday School, and classes. To prepare for the conversation, read one chapter of this book each weekday, Monday through Friday.

- Week 1: read 1 through 5.
- Week 2: read 6 through 10.
- Week 3: read 11 through 15.
- Week 4: read 16 through 20.
- Week 5: read 21 through 25.
- Week 6: read 26 through 30.
- Week 7: read 31 through 35.
- Week 8: read 36 through 40.

When you get together, discuss the questions at the end of each chapter. The leader can use all the questions to guide your discussion or pick which ones to focus on.

Before you begin, pray as a group. Ask for Holy Spirit insight and clarity.

As you consider each chapter's questions:

- Look for how this can grow your understanding of the Bible.
- Evaluate how this can expand your faith perspective.
- Consider what you need to change in how you live your lives.

End by asking God to help apply what you've learned.

May God bless you as you read and study his Word.

IF YOU'RE NEW TO THE BIBLE

Each entry in this book contains Bible references. These can guide you if you want to learn more. If you're not familiar with the Bible, here's an overview to get you started, give some context, and minimize confusion.

First, the Bible is a collection of works written by various authors over several centuries. Think of the Bible as a diverse anthology of godly communication. It contains historical accounts, poetry, songs, letters of instruction and encouragement, messages from God sent through his representatives, and prophecies.

Most versions of the Bible have sixty-six books grouped into two sections: The Old Testament and the New Testament. The Old Testament contains thirty-nine books that precede and anticipate Jesus. The New Testament includes twenty-seven books and covers Jesus's life and the work of his followers.

The reference notations in the Bible, such as Romans 3:23, are analogous to line numbers in a Shakespearean play. They serve as a study aid. Since the Bible is much longer and more complex than a play, its reference notations are more involved.

As already mentioned, the Bible is an amalgam of books, or sections, such as Genesis, Psalms, or Matthew. These are the names given to them, over time, based on the piece's author, audience, or purpose.

In the 1200s, each book was divided into chapters, such as Acts 2 or Psalm 23. In the 1500s, the chapters were further subdivided into verses, such as John 3:16. Let's use this as an example.

The name of the book (John) appears first, followed by the chapter number (3), a colon, and then the verse number (16). Sometimes called a chapter-verse reference notation, this helps people quickly find a specific text regardless of their version of the Bible.

Although the goal was to place these chapter and verse divisions at logical breaks, they sometimes seem arbitrary. Therefore, it's good practice to read what precedes and follows each passage you're studying. The text before or after it may contain relevant insights into the portion you're exploring.

Here's how to look up a specific passage in the Bible based on its reference: Most Bibles contain a table of contents, which gives the page number for the beginning of each book. Start there. Locate the book you want to read, and turn to that page. Then flip forward to the chapter you want. Last, skim that chapter to locate the specific verse.

If you want to read online, enter the reference into BibleGateway.com or BibleHub.com. Also check out the YouVersion app.

Learn more about the greatest book ever written at ABibleADay.com, which provides a Bible blog, summaries of the books of the Bible, a dictionary of Bible terms, Bible reading plans, and other resources.

ABOUT PETER DEHAAN

Peter DeHaan, PhD, wants to change the world one word at a time. His books and blog posts discuss God, the Bible, and church, geared toward spiritual seekers and church dropouts. Many people feel church has let them down, and Peter seeks to encourage them as they search for a place to belong.

But he's not afraid to ask tough questions or make religious people squirm. He's not trying to be provocative. Instead, he seeks truth, even if it makes people uncomfortable. Peter urges Christians to push past the status quo and reexamine how they practice their faith in every part of their lives.

Peter earned his doctorate, awarded with high distinction, from Trinity College of the Bible and Theological Seminary. He lives with his wife in beautiful Southwest Michigan and wrangles crossword puzzles in his spare time.

A lifelong student of Scripture, Peter wrote the 1,000-page website ABibleADay.com to encourage people to explore the Bible, the greatest book ever written. His popular blog, at PeterDeHaan.com, addresses biblical Christianity to build a faith that matters.

Read his blog, receive his newsletter, and learn more at PeterDeHaan.com.

BOOKS BY PETER DEHAAN

40-Day Bible Study Series

Dear Theophilus (the Gospel of Luke, formerly That You May Know)

Dear Theophilus, Acts (formerly Tongues of Fire)

Dear Theophilus, Isaiah (formerly For Unto Us)

Dear Theophilus, Minor Prophets (formerly Return to Me)

Dear Theophilus, Job (formerly I Hope in Him)

Living Water (the Gospel of John)

Love Is Patient (Paul's letters to the Corinthians)

Revelation Bible Study (formerly A New Heaven and a New Earth)

Love One Another (John's letters)

Run with Perseverance (the book of Hebrews)

James and Jude Bible Study

Matthew Bible Study

Mark Bible Study (available in 2025)

Holiday Celebration Series

The Advent of Jesus

The Passion of Jesus (Lent)

The Victory of Jesus (Easter

The Ministry of Jesus

Bible Character Sketches Series

Women of the Bible

The Friends and Foes of Jesus

Old Testament Sinners and Saints

More Old Testament Sinners and Saints

Heroes and Heavies of the Apocrypha

200 Old Testament Sinners and Saints

Visiting Churches Series

52 Churches

The 52 Churches Workbook

More Than 52 Churches

The More Than 52 Churches Workbook

Shopping for Church

Visiting Online Church

Other Books

Jesus's Broken Church

Martin Luther's 95 Theses (formerly *95 Tweets*)

The Christian Church's LGBTQ Failure

Bridging the Sacred-Secular Divide (formerly *Woodpecker Wars*)

Beyond Psalm 150

How Big Is Your Tent?

Elephant God (available in 2025)

For the latest list of all Peter's books, go to PeterDeHaan.com/books.